Books,
Libraries
and Electronics
Essays on the Future
of Written Communication

by
Efrem Sigel
Erik Barnouw
Anthony Smith
Dan Lacy
Robert D. Stueart
Lewis M. Branscomb

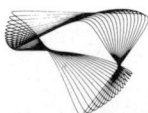

Knowledge Industry Publications, Inc.
White Plains, NY and London

Communications Library

Books, Libraries and Electronics: Essays on the Future of Written Communication

Library of Congress Cataloging in Publication Data

Main entry under title:
Books, libraries and electronics.

(Communications library)
Bibliography: p.
Includes index.
1. Electronics in libraries—Addresses, essays, lectures. 2. Electronics in printing—Addresses, essays, lectures. I. Sigel, Efrem. II. Series.
Z678.9.B64   025.3′ 028′54   82-15229
ISBN 0-86729-024-2   AACR2

Printed in the United States of America

10   9   8   7   6   5   4   3   2   1

Table of Contents

Foreword

The six important essays that here await the reader explore the rich and varied world of communication, offering fresh insights into a complex theme and documenting how different media serve specific needs and complement other technologies. Does it matter *how* we receive our information and become knowledgeable? Of course it does. A person's ability to imagine and to select what is needed or wanted from the vast outpouring of creative minds all over the world is increasingly important. Changing printing and publishing technologies and life styles impel us to adjust to and select from a splendid array of information carriers.

Acquiring knowledge is hard work; it takes time and an inquiring mind, and differs considerably from picking up bits and pieces of information that may be immediately and randomly useful. This volume reminds us how remarkable it is that I can learn and you can learn, neither of us subtracting from the world of knowledge, each becoming more capable of adding to it. We are blessed with an exploring spirit and an incredible array of vehicles to select for our excursions of the mind.

Each day at the Library of Congress, I pass the Gutenberg Bible, on display in the Great Hall. This is enroute to the Computer Cataloging Center (which is not far from the Microfilm Reading Room), in the same building that houses many of the 18 million books in the collections of "America's Library." Here, at least, there is no reason to ask, "Is the book dead?" The supposed contest among the media is a myth; each has its uses and users. After reading this book, I think the vote is in. Books will survive, and so will many other forms of communication, some familiar, others yet unimagined. I am exhilarated by the prospects and by the prospecting.

Carol A. Nemeyer
Associate Librarian for National Programs
The Library of Congress

The Center for the Book

What is the Center for the Book? Why is it a part of the Library of Congress, the world's largest library? In the words of Daniel J. Boorstin, the Librarian of Congress, the goal of the Center for the Book is "to keep the book flourishing." Established in October 1977 by an Act of Congress, the Center is a catalyst among authors, publishers, booksellers, librarians, educators, business leaders, scholars and *readers*. With the assistance of a National Advisory Board made up of prominent representatives from the book, educational and business communities, the Center serves a diverse constituency through an active program of special events to organize, focus and dramatize the nation's interest in books, reading and the printed word. In planning for the establishment of the Center, Dr. Boorstin explained why it should be in the Library of Congress:

> As the national library of a great free republic we have a special interest to see that books do not go unread, that they are read by people of all ages and conditions, that books are not buried in their own dross, not lost from neglect nor obscured from us by specious alternatives and synthetic substances. As the national library of the most technologically advanced nation on earth, we have a special duty, too, to see that the book is the useful, illuminating servant of all other technologies, and that all other technologies become the effective, illuminating acolytes of the book.

True to its catalytic function, the Center has a full-time staff of only two people, and its programs are entirely supported by private contributions.

Knowledge Industry Publications Inc. will contribute to this effort by donating royalties from the sale of this volume to the Center. These funds will help make possible special seminars, symposia, lectures and exhibitions celebrating the role of the book in our culture. We hope that this model expression of private sector support will inspire other publishers and authors.

Carol A. Nemeyer

1

The Future of the Book

by Efrem Sigel

For much of their history, books have been controversial because of their content. From Galileo, Voltaire and Tom Paine to Darwin, Marx and Solzhenitsin, the ideas contained in books have helped shake the Church, topple monarchies, spread the idea of independence or revolution, usher in a new way of looking at the world. *Candide*, *Common Sense*, *Origin of Species*, *Das Kapital*, *Gulag Archipelago*—all were testimony to the power of the book to nudge or propel society in new directions. But in the last part of the 20th century a different sort of controversy surrounds the book. It has to do not with the content of books, but with their form. In an age when new electronic channels of communication are taking hold, the question being heard is: Will the book survive?

The television set and the computer epitomize the electronic challenge to books—and by extension, to publishers and libraries. Television already occupies six to seven hours a day in the average American household. With the addition of video cassette recorders, video disc players and cable TV systems offering 80 channels, TV has the potential to be even more widely used. As for computers, they have progressed from giant machines of use only in scientific calculations, to portable devices within economic reach of every small business, every school, even every household.

The marriage of computers with television, moreover, makes possible communications systems that are flexible and speedy, and that compete directly with the printed page as a means of displaying text. Computer-controlled video discs can store the contents of thousands of books on a thin plastic sphere; specially adapted TV sets can call up millions of pages of text from remote data banks; personal computers can be programmed to compose and send letters electronically; satellites can carry video or computer teleconferences that take the place of written messages, phone calls and personal visits.

All these technologies pose a threat to print in general and to the book in particular—but then, so have many other inventions of the past 100 years, from telephone and telegraph to radio, movies and phonograph. To answer the question "Does the book have a future?" requires an understanding of processes rather than physical products. It is the process of publishing that results in books being produced; it is the process of acquiring information—for education, for work, for personal enrichment and relaxation—that results in their being bought. Only by examining these processes in the light of new electronic technologies can we appreciate the changes in store for the book.

PERSISTENCE OF PRINTED PUBLICATIONS: THE NEWSPAPER CASE

One of the first applications of electronic technology to publishing is to streamline the production of existing printed materials. The newspaper industry illustrates this point aptly. During the 1970s the daily paper underwent a revolution in production technology as fundamental as that affecting any industry. The letterpress printing process gave way increasingly to offset lithography. Slow and bulky hot metal linotype machines went the way of the blacksmith shop, to be replaced by faster, noiseless photocomposition equipment. By the end of the decade many newspapers had completely shut down their composing rooms; reporters using video display terminals and editors using electronic editing consoles were doing the writing, correcting and composition. This changeover to electronic technology—made possible by powerful computer systems for storing and manipulating text, as well as for driving the photocomposition machines—will soon result in full-page makeup systems that do away with all manual handling of type. The conversion has involved an investment by the newspaper industry running into the billions of dollars in the past dozen years.

The curious thing about this process is that it has been accomplished without any change in the appearance of the daily paper. Like the electronic revolution in banking and brokerage houses—which involves almost complete computer processing of transactions—the newspaper revolution has remained a back-office phenomenon. The ultimate product remains the printed paper, just as the product of a bank or stock transaction remains a check or a printed account statement.

Why this is so for newspapers is a complex mixture of economics, tradition and consumer preference. Getting 40,000 or so daily newspaper reporters to write their stories on video terminals may have been a difficult feat, but it is utterly trivial compared to the problem of getting 62 million newspaper buyers to forego the printed paper in favor of an electronic version.

The daily newspaper combines in its 60 or 96 pages so many different functions—news source, reports of yesterday's stock prices, offerings of houses and jobs, coffee and frozen foods coupons—that it is difficult to envision its complete replacement by any electronic alternative.

What has happened, however, is that computerizing the

production of the daily paper and of related news services has made it possible to offer bits and pieces of the information through interactive retrieval systems. This explains the development of services like the New York Times Information Bank, Dow Jones News Retrieval, The Source and NEXIS. The market for these services, some of which charge $60 or more per hour, is a small community of business, government and academic customers, numbering in the tens of thousands today, and it has in no way disturbed the attachment of millions of readers to their daily paper.

At some point, of course, those functions of the newspaper that can most benefit from computer searching may begin to disappear from the printed page; included in this category might be certain classified ads, listings, commodity prices, etc.

Book publishers are far behind newspaper publishers in their application of computers to production. No books require the fast turnaround time of the daily paper; as a result no book publishers maintain the sort of investment in typesetting and printing facilities common at newspapers. Almost all publishers rely on outside typesetters and printers. Nevertheless, computers, photocomposition equipment and word processors are beginning to make their way into publishing houses—typically, those that produce scientific, technical and professional books, as well as texts. As more of the content of books is captured in machine-readable form, derivative uses, e.g., through online computer searching, will become possible. If the newspaper industry is any guide, it will take five to 10 years for the equipment to become widely dispersed, but this does not mean that certain publishers won't move much faster. The major obstacle to computerizing the production process is that with books, unlike newspapers, manuscripts are created by independent authors, not by staff employees. Already, however, some publishers are lending authors word processors so the original manuscript can be created in a machine-readable version, thus speeding up subsequent editing and typesetting.

THE ELECTRONIC VISION AND PUBLISHING REALITY

The lesson of the newspaper is important for all who deal in the writing, editing, publishing and collecting of books. Using computers has automated one aspect of newspaper publishing, while leaving untouched such varied activities as: the speed at which reporters can think and write, the problems of selling advertising, or the dependence on truck drivers and 12-year-old delivery boys to get the paper to the doorstep.

Yet when it comes to books, one of the persistent myths of online computer retrieval systems is that they will streamline the publication of information by miraculously circumventing everything that happens in between the time the writer gets up from his typewriter, and the moment the reader sits down with the printed book. What happens in between, of course, is the publishing process, consisting, in simplified form, of four distinct phases: 1) editing, revision and preparation for publication; 2) composition, or creation of a master image for printing; 3) printing or other mechanical reproduction; and 4) marketing and physical distribution to the consumers of information.

The vision of an all-electronic system for disseminating information often finds expression in a series of "if only" wishes expressed by the intelligent, albeit naive, observer of the publishing world. The wish list goes something like this:

"If only writers were equipped with terminals (word processors, microcomputers or whatever) for the creation of text..."

"If only libraries could get away from their preoccupation with physical collections of publications, and would concentrate instead on facilitating the retrieval of information from remote data banks..."

"And if only information users [formerly known as readers] were equipped with, and disposed to use, terminals for the retrieval of text..."

...then, say the seers, the information millennium would be

upon us. Publication of everything would take place nearly instantaneously. Authors, publishers and readers anywhere in the world could communicate with one another electronically. And costs would be lower. No editors, no typesetters, no printers, no marketing organizations, no bookstores and newsstands would stand between the creators and users of information. Both the distribution of information and the payment for it would take place at the punch of a button, and everyone would gain: writers, consumers, schools and libraries, and society at large.

Publisher as Processor

In this stirring, if misguided, concept of how information gets to its intended audience, the role of the publisher is reduced to that of the typesetter, printer and trucking company: The publisher simply processes manuscripts, turning them into finished products we now know as books, journals, magazines and newspapers, but that we could just as easily know in a different, electronic form.

Yet the most important activity a publisher performs is that involving manuscripts that never get published. He does this by saying no. Critics of our publishing process lament the publication of 45,000 books a year (actually, the number is probably twice as high) but ignore the far greater number of outlines, sample chapters and complete manuscripts that never become books, thanks to the obstinacy of publishers and their refusal to mechanically turn into a book every idea that crosses their desks.

Publisher as Gatekeeper

It is this facet of publishing, acknowledged but rarely understood by outsiders, that gives rise to a second, equally persistent notion: the publisher as gatekeeper. Academic observers of publishing, like sociologist Lewis Coser, have emphasized this concept. Although the term gatekeeper need not be pejorative, it certainly conjures up an image of publishers as cultural potentates who, by the exercise of personal whim or class judgment, decide which writers may see their works in print and what the audience for books may read.

The vision of electronic publishing that would have information go from the author to the computer to the reader pays scant heed to this gatekeeper aspect of publishing, considering it trivial. No need for gatekeepers, say the visionaries. In the technological democracy of electronic information transfer, writers will write what they want, readers will read what they want, and nothing need intervene.

One of the most eloquent spokesmen for this vision of the future is F.W. Lancaster at the University of Illinois. "Whether we like it or not," he writes, "print on paper will eventually give way completely to electronics, at least for those publications designed primarily to transmit factual information, rather than to entertain or 'inspire.' " The scientist of 20 years hence will scan and create all information at his terminal.

When such a scientist is ready to publish his work, Lancaster writes, "he submits his article to the editor of an electronic journal....All communication among author, editor and referees is electronic. This communication is rapid and needed changes are very easily made."[1]

Though conceding in passing that editors will continue to exist (though he says nothing about publishers per se), Lancaster otherwise envisions technology as curing human laziness and obliterating the inevitable tensions that accom-

---

1. F.W. Lancaster, "The Future of the Library in the Age of Telecommunications," in *Telecommunications and Libraries: A Primer for Librarians and Information Managers*, by Donald W. King, F.W. Lancaster, Brigitte Kenney, et al. (White Plains, NY: Knowledge Industry Publications, Inc., 1981), p. 147.

pany publishing work, or any other work. We need to be skeptical about these unstated assumptions. Is it believable that authors, editors, reviewers and readers will instantly respond to mail and comments simply because those comments are delivered at the speed of light? Or that there will be no disagreements between authors and editors? Or that editors will never have to say "no" to a submission to the electronic journal because the incredibly low costs of disk storage mean that everything can be accepted?

Or is it possible that the process of selecting material for publication—and of revising what needs revision—will become even more complex, in some ways even slower than today, simply because it becomes cheaper and easier to submit such material electronically than in typewritten form? (True, the computer is a superhighway for moving information. But the building of a superhighway sometimes increases traffic so much that even this roadway gets clogged.)

PHOTOCOPIERS AND PUBLISHING

Actually, if the ideal for information transfer is quick, direct communication between authors and readers, there is no need to wait for all-digital systems. An excellent medium for low-cost, rapid, selective transfer of information has existed since 1960. Its creator was not IBM but Xerox.

The photocopier using plain paper, simple enough to be operated by a five-year-old (not to mention by a writer or editor), should in theory have been an enormous boon to reading, writing and publishing. A 200-page manuscript that the author types himself, or has prepared by a professional typist, can be duplicated in quantities of a couple of hundred for as little as $6 per copy. The whole job takes only a few hours and there is no need to deal with publisher, typesetter or printer. The completed copies can be punched or stapled or enclosed in a plastic binder and distributed in whatever way is appropriate: given away one at a time, sold in Harvard Square or on the Berkeley campus, sent via mail to paying customers, even shipped to bookstores for re-sale.

Why, then, has the photocopier not spurred a revolution in publishing, whether of the do-it-yourself, not-for-profit or highly specialized commercial variety?

To some extent it has. There is more self-publishing in the age of Xerox and of rapid photo-offset printing. Everything from office memos to technical reports to political manifestos can be copied at the push of the "print" button. But copies made is not the same as copies read. And most of us would concede that along with its undoubted, even essential contribution to information transfer, the photocopying machine has heightened the problem of dealing with information by creating millions or billions of copies that no one needs to, or cares to, read.

When entering information into the computer is as simple as pressing the copying machine button, and when the cost of storing a page for a year on computer disk is less than the cost of a sheet of paper, can anyone doubt the result will be the same: billions of pages of information that no one needs?

But who decides what anyone needs to read?

THE ESSENCE OF PUBLISHING

Ultimately, we each decide that for ourselves, by choosing among publications available, or seeking out what we want. The peculiar contribution of the publisher is to facilitate this choice by guessing what we want and risking his money, or his company's money, to make it available to us. It is the interplay between the wants and needs of the audience and the judgment of the publisher in interpreting those wants that is the essence of publishing.

The term "gatekeeper" notwithstanding, no one licenses publishers in 20th century America or Britain or France. Publishing is not a profession or guild, but a business open to anyone with capital to risk and ideas to test. Of course, publishers and editors influence tastes, or better, anticipate tastes by deciding what to publish; but they cannot override those tastes. (The bigger the publisher, the more expensive is this lesson. Time Inc., one of the world's largest, relearns it every decade. In 1972 it shut down *Life* as a weekly; in 1981 it closed the doors on the daily Washington *Star*—in both cases after many millions of dollars in losses.)

Marketing of Publications

In an electronic age of push-button access to information, the economics of the publisher's role may change dramatically. But the linchpin of that role—deciding what to publish and how to reach the audience—will not change. Storing large amounts of text in a computer or on a video disc will cut the cost of distributing publications, especially those of short length or limited audience. This could lower the breakeven point for certain titles, whether single articles or monographs, thus making possible greater output. But the cost of marketing these electronic publications will not decrease, and very likely will increase. Since the amount of time available to readers will not expand, it will be an even harder job than it is now to bring a given work to the attention of its intended audience.

Importance of Imprimatur

Whether the form of a publication is a bound book or a series of frames on a video display terminal, a publisher's imprimatur will be desirable, if not essential. The reason that the photocopied manuscript distributed up and down Fifth Avenue and 57th Street does not carry the same authority as a jacketed book in the Doubleday Store, a hundred yards away, has to do of course with physical appearance but in more important measure with this matter of imprimatur. When the publisher stands between the author and the reader, the author's work takes on added authority—in part because of editorial revisions, in part because of the mere fact that it has been selected.

Although imprimatur can exist with electronic publishing, no one knows exactly how this will work. For the time being, a serious problem with furnishing information over a video screen—a problem that is psychological as well as tangible—is that the uniform appearance of the display tends to give all material equal weight. It is far more difficult for a publisher to establish the look and feel of his book or journal electronically than in print. In the latter case, he has page size, type selection, logo, layout and cover to work with. The problem of imprimatur is most acute where a single computer service offers information from many different publishers and authors. In such a system, ten lines from an obscure directory or a regional magazine do not look very different from ten lines plucked out of *Time* magazine. At present, both author and publisher will resist this sort of homogenization and loss of recognition; in the future, of course, technology will permit far more variation in electronic display than has been possible heretofore.

Self-publishing, then, will no more be a hallmark of computer-based systems than it is of print and video communications media. True, the coming of the low-cost video recorder and camera (discussed in Erik Barnouw's essay) and the coming of Xerox have both been a spur to self-expression, one for television, the other for print. But commercial publishing has flourished in the age of the photocopier, just as commercial television has flourished in the age of Sony.

The same reasons of economics and imprimatur that persuade writers to continue to give their work to commercial publishers, instead of publishing it themselves, will hold sway if and when the computer is widely used as a printing press.

READERS AND CHOICE

Writers and publishers are two of the links in the publishing chain. But what of the reader? Without readers who show their approval of what is published by paying money for it, the publishing enterprise sputters and stops.

Viewed from afar, readers seem to be merely passive recipients of what is published: they accept or reject, but they do not influence. This is a superficial perspective, however. Readers are in reality anything but passive. The great variety of publications available enables readers to vote with their time and their wallets. This voting is most visible when it comes to the 15 bestselling fiction and nonfiction titles reported every week on *The New York Times* bestseller list. These are books that can sell 100,000 to 200,000 copies in hardcover or 1 million to 2 million in paperback in the course of a year.

But when it comes to the more specialized books—40,000 of which get published every year—there is no scorecard like the *Times* bestseller list to measure reader taste.

How, then, do readers communicate to publishers at large what they want to read? And how, short of the most wasteful process of trial and error, do publishers divine what their readers desire?

In part, of course, this process of trial and error does determine what gets published; whether it is in fact wasteful depends on the alternatives that exist for obtaining reader feedback. The long answer is that in an information-rich society like the United States, or in other industrialized countries, readers communicate their wants in all sorts of ways—by professional concerns, by the movies and television programs they watch, by the plays and concerts they attend, by the records they buy, by the sports teams they root for, by the athletic and leisure activities they engage in. If publishing is to succeed it must be a mirror of society's activities, hobbies, business and professional pursuits, intellectual endeavors and political concerns. Not that there can be *one* such mirror, or, more precisely, not that such a mirror can be without many facets. But the more diversity exists in the activities and interests of a society, the more diversity must exist in its publications—in all forms, print (newspapers, magazines, books) as well as audiovisual or electronic.

Moreover, the cross-echos between activities and information, and between diverse information sources, can be extremely complex. Books may stimulate producers to commission screenwriters to do screenplays that become movies; the movies in turn are shown on TV; sometimes they spawn TV series, which in turn lead to new books. Any popular idea may turn into a book; any popular book will attract imitators on the same subject. This process is very visible where books on running or yoga or assertiveness or money seem to come in endless waves. But it operates equally well in the competitive world of scholarly, technical and professional publishing.

The process certainly has its profligate aspects, but on balance I believe strongly that it is profoundly healthy for a society—particularly one that prizes democracy and freedom of expression.

What corrects the process, and keeps it in check, is the choice exercised by consumers of books, the readers. Unless publishers exhibit judgment in choosing what to publish (the gatekeeper role), skill in editing what is submitted, and competence in reaching the intended audience (in other words, unless they do a good job of marketing), their books will fail. So, ultimately, will the companies that issue them. This is the ultimate feedback—one, unfortunately, from which there is no reprieve.

Thus, just as publishers make many thousands of individual decisions on what to publish, readers make individual decisions on what to read and what to buy. The readers' decisions number well over a billion, however, since nearly 1.7 billion copies are purchased annually in the U.S., each the result of a conscious choice. From the inside of such an industry, the activity appears random, frenetic and totally unpredictable. From the outside, or viewed over a period of years, it develops rhythms, logic and direction.

Ultimately, the future of the book depends more on what readers want than on what publishers try. Publishers will respond to public demands for information in whatever form the public wants it. This fact explains the proliferation of titles referred to earlier. And it foreshadows, as well, the inevitable diversification of publishers into new electronic media. The fruits of this diversification are either to fall to existing companies or, if they refuse to act to satisfy customer wants, to newer companies that grow up around newer media.

THE CURRENT MARKET FOR BOOKS

To guess what the future of the book will be in an electronic age, it is necessary to look at the present state of book publishing. The distribution of book sales falls into three broad categories:

1) books sold primarily to individual consumers
2) books sold to professional and business customers
3) books sold to educational institutions

In the first category are sales of trade and religious books; mass market paperbacks; book club and mail order titles. This is by far the largest segment of the publishing industry, representing $3.5 billion in publishers' domestic sales in 1980. In the second category are technical, medical, and business, legal and other professional books, as well as university press titles, a grouping that accounted for $890 million in publishers' U.S. sales in 1980. The final category, consisting of school and college texts, standardized tests and related audiovisual materials, had sales of around $2 billion in 1980.

Another way of looking at this sales distribution is by units rather than dollars. Although these figures must be estimates, because of the difficulty of obtaining accurate industry-wide figures on units sold, one tabulation suggests the following distribution for 1980: books sold to consumers, 1.29 billion units; books sold to professional customers, 61 million units; books sold to educational institutions and students, 347 million units.

The dominance of the consumer segment of book publishing stands out even more clearly when measured in units. This segment accounted for 55% of dollar sales but more than 75% of unit sales. The overriding reason is the mass market paperback, which accounts for $679 million in sales but 534 million units, nearly a third of industry shipments. Both of the other categories have a far higher share of dollar sales than of units: educational books account for 31% of the industry in dollars, but only 20% in units. Professional books represent 14% of the dollar sales but a meager 3.6% of units.

Consumer Books

Although a portion of consumer books are sold to libraries and educational institutions, the overwhelming share goes to individuals. It's fair to conclude, then, that most of the books sold in the United States go to satisfy the desires of people for diversion, information and self-fulfillment. The next largest number of books is for the formal education of students in schools and colleges. And the smallest number—though by no means an insignificant portion, in either dollars or units— goes to convey professional information.

In the consumer market, books must compete against all other forms of leisure time activities, some quite expensive (like round the world tours, or skiing in Innsbruck), and some virtually costless (like watching television or walking in the park). This competition for leisure time acts to keep the price of books low, compared to almost any other way of distributing information. A 300-page paperback bestseller sells for $3.95, or 1.3 cents per page; the cost per thousand words works out to be about 3.1 cents. By comparison, duplicating your own typed manuscript at the local photo-copying shop will cost you 15 cents per thousand words; talking on the telephone will cost $2 per thousand words; sending a message via telex will cost about $5 per thousand words. And retrieving information from a computerized data bank like The Source will cost $5 to $8 per thousand words during business hours, though only a third of that at night.

This elemental economic fact, combined with the portability and physical attractiveness of books, guarantees that they will be an item desired by millions of consumers for many years to come. Indeed, given the present state of technology for distributing information electronically, it is difficult to conceive of any computer-based system that can challenge the book for recreational reading, whether at home, on the train or at the beach.

Professional Books

A very different state of affairs prevails for professional reading, however. Many professional books are consulted rather than read; they are a means of acquiring specific information when desired. The marketing handbook is consulted when its owner needs to engage a research firm; the medical text is referred to when the physician encounters an unusual problem; the book of engineering formulas is a repository of calculations needed by the structural engineer when he measures the stress of a new building.

All these uses are conceivable from a computerized data base that supplies facts on request to a video screen. In many cases such a display is the preferred choice. Why plow through line after close line of names and addresses, looking for a desired phone number, when just the name being sought could flash onto a screen? Why search through shelves or roomfuls of legal texts for just the right precedent, when a computer search can turn up all 96 cases that bear on the disputed point?

The professional doing research has no great loyalty to the

book as a physical form; it is the information he is seeking. Many types of material will still require the close reading that is only possible with the printed page, of course. If the reader is seeking not an answer to a market research problem but Peter Drucker's insights into modern management, then the best way to acquire those insights is to plunk down in the armchair and read.

BOOKS AND READING

Considered in this way, it becomes obvious that reading has many different purposes. Reading a number in the telephone directory is akin to reading a street sign or a price tag: it is a pointer, a visual aid to an item of information. Once the information is acquired, the person goes on to the next act: making a phone call, a left turn, or the purchase of a pair of boots.

The rapid reading of the daily paper or an industry trade magazine is quite a different matter; here the individual is engaged in scanning a large amount of information, familiarizing himself with events, assimilating facts and opinion about the state of the world, his neighborhood, his customers.

Then there is the reading of a novel or book of popular nonfiction: the way words are put together, the flow of the story, the description of characters—all these aspects of a book transport the reader, stimulate the imagination and give a rich pleasure.

Different, too, is the close reading of a text or other serious work to acquire knowledge—whether the knowledge is the foundation of biochemistry or the grammar of French. This sort of reading goes slowly, is combined with other activities— lectures, lab exercises—demands repetition, and if properly done results in the most significant change in behavior: the ability to do something new.

Books can facilitate all four types of reading, but it's apparent that in the first sort the reader will have no great loyalty to the book as object. In the second type, print in general still has great advantages over electronic alternatives, although it is conceivable that the computer and the video screen will eventually find a way of filling certain of these needs. It is in the third and fourth spheres that the book still reigns. If a form of entertainment is to challenge the printed word it will be—as historically it has been—an audiovisual one like movies, television and radio, not a display of text over a terminal. As for formal education, at every level it relies on the text as the bedrock of organized knowledge. The slide, the video tape may supplement the text in important ways but they will not replace it.

If these are the kinds of books, and the kinds of reading that go with them, it becomes much harder to answer the question: "What becomes of the book in an electronic age?" Precisely because it is not *the* book, but thousands of books that are published every year, half a million in print today, billions of copies in circulation—all going to satisfy the needs of millions of readers.

Of all the communications media, the book remains the most versatile, issued in the greatest variety of sizes, formats, print runs and prices. One title, a mass market paperback, is printed on the lowest cost paper available, priced at $3.50 and sells to 6 million customers. Another, a limited-edition facsimile of Leonardo drawings, is treated like a work of art (which it is), designed and printed on the finest paper, bound by hand in leather, produced in an edition of a few hundred copies, and priced at $1000. In between these two examples are books on all subjects and for all tastes, in prices ranging from a few dollars to hundreds of dollars, and in printings that go as high as many millions and as low as 100.

FUTURE OF THE LIBRARY

The same dilemma applies when we go beyond the book to

ask, "What is the future of the library that collects the book in an electronic age?"

Just as there are many types of books, there are many types of libraries. And each type, in turn, collects different books. The public library's mainstay is popular fiction and nonfiction, along with a few hundred current magazines. But the public library also maintains classics of literature, self-study texts on everything from boating to zoology, records and tapes. The academic or research library, while offering these same resources, adds many thousands of scholarly books and journals, as well as access to computerized search services or other special research activities. It may also house non-Western language collections, archives of historic papers and original manuscripts. The special library in law or medicine or technology provides resources in its particular field.

In the same way that electronic technology forces us to confront the distinction between books as physical objects and books as information carriers, technology also requires us to distinguish between the library as a building and the library as an intellectual scheme for organizing and making available information. Lancaster, in his vision of the transition from a paper-based to an electronic-based society, sees the physical library as all but doomed:

"...as the electronic sources continue to gain in importance, and the paper sources decline, as terminals become more common in offices and in homes, and as individual researchers become familiar and comfortable with the use of online data bases, the need for these researchers to visit libraries will rapidly diminish. When this occurs, the library as an institution will begin its inevitable decline." [2]

At the same time, Lancaster foresees an enhanced role for the librarian as information specialist: once librarians have cut their ties to the institution, they can act as information

2. Ibid., p. 151.

consultants, analysts, members of a research team, etc., and thus enjoy "responsibilities far beyond those they have at present."[3]

This provocative forecast has a great deal of logic behind it, but its sweeping character does not do justice to the complexity of library activities and clientele. It may be entirely possible to replace certain functions of the academic or industrial research library with electronic access to technical literature. But millions of people use the public library every day for purposes as varied as doing research for a high school assignment, collecting the latest James Michener novel, copying down plans for a do-it-yourself piece of furniture, borrowing a record or tape (and soon, a video tape or a personal computer program), and having a warm place to read, study or snooze. Nothing on the horizon can supplant the role of the public library in lending popular fiction and nonfiction, nor is there any reason to dispense with its other, more social functions merely because computers or video media can satisfy certain specific needs for reference information.

A more plausible prediction than Lancaster's, at least for several generations, is for a rich interplay between the library as physical repository and new electronic means of distributing information. Online catalogs of local library holdings, accessible by phone lines or by cable television, can make patrons' use of the physical library more efficient, by telling them in advance whether a desired book is available. Mail or electronic delivery of certain publications could save a trip to the library altogether, perhaps leading to consolidation of certain branches. Or, totally mechanized systems of borrowing and returning books could lead to the establishment of automated branches which, like automated teller machines

---

3. Ibid., p. 152 .

(ATMs) in the banking industry, could dispense books 24 hours a day.

(Such machines, modeled after vending machines, might hold 100 paperbacks each, and after the patron had entered his library card number and the computer had verified it, the desired title would slide down the chute into the patron's hands, along with a printed slip telling the date it must be returned. Patrons might even pay an annual deposit to use the system; the money would be refundable on request, but interest on the funds would help support the upkeep of these automated branches.)

Many other possibilities exist; the point is that libraries have barely begun to envision how computer and other electronic technologies can extend their role, deepening patron loyalty and making scarce funds work harder than they do today.

Moreover, there is one function of the library that is so tied to the printed book that it is inconceivable it will ever wither away.

This is the library's role as preserver of the past. Libraries collectively house centuries of human expression: books and periodicals from every period and in every language, running to billions of pages and trillions of words. There is no way in the foreseeable future to convert more than the tiniest fraction of this treasure into computerized form. (Even the effort to convert the millions of pre-1970s catalog records held at the Library of Congress to machine-readable form foundered because of the immense size and cost of the project.)

Only in science and technology is it true that most searches for information can be satisfied by material that has been published in the last five years. In religion, history, philosophy, literature, what was published 300 or 2000 years ago may be more important—even more in demand—than what was published last week. One has only to compare annual sales of the Bible to sales of last year's bestseller, or compare annual circulation of a public library's copy of *War and Peace* to its circulation of the latest Harold Robbins novel, to recognize this truth. The role of the physical library in making the past accessible to us will continue not out of sterile tradition, but because it is alive; technology offers no ready alternative.

BOOKS, LIBRARIES AND ELECTRONICS: FORM AND SUBSTANCE

It is in contemplating the book as physical object and the library as physical repository that we can perhaps draw a bit closer to what the future will bring. There is no substitute for the collective treasure represented by books published years or even centuries ago. Nor is there, today, a substitute for issuing popular new titles in this format: the printed and bound book is too convenient, low-cost, portable and familiar to yield to any electronic surrogate.

But these uses of books and libraries do not tell us everything. Some functions of the book, like reference, look-up or tutoring, are better handled by computer access, by audiovisual display, or by a combination of printed and electronic means. Other functions, like diversion and enter-tainment, are not unique to books. Movies and TV perform these functions now, while new media like cable television, video cassettes, video games are developing rapidly. Looking at the panoply of new information media available, any dispassionate observer must conclude not that books will disappear, but that their claim on our attention and pocket-books will diminish in the future. This does not mean that the book publishing industry will shrink in size; it will continue to grow, but will form a smaller part of the overall com-munications environment. Such a change is not new. It has been in progress for much of this century.

As discussed earlier, electronic technologies offer many possibilities for improving the publication of books in printed form, as well as the way libraries serve their patrons today. Once this has been said, however, it must also be recognized that both publishing and libraries have a mission that is not synonymous with the future of the book. To publish is to make available information for every human need—education, inspiration, entertainment, commerce, science. There is no way such a mission can be limited to issuing books; if today's publishers do not seize the opportunity presented by electronic media, new publishers will inevitably arise to do so.

The same is true of libraries. Even today, although books are their most visible offering, these institutions provide access to records, tapes, movies, lectures, concerts and online computer searches. As new communications forms evolve, libraries must evolve with them. Otherwise their role as archives of the past—which today is just one of many important roles—will become central, thus dooming the library to a shrunken place in the communications world.

For many years, books themselves will continue to be published by the tens of thousands, bought by the hundreds of millions, or billions. They will remain highly familiar objects, not relics of the past. But as the landscape of communications changes, so will their role, and our perception of it. The evolution of that landscape will be very gradual but persistent, and one of its distinguishing features in the 21st century will be that those involved in communications will no longer consider it a question of the moment to ask, "Does the book have a future?"

2

Video and the Printed Word

by Erik Barnouw

Television's influence on the domain of print is full of contradictions and surprises. But we can be sure it is far-reaching, with indirect effects on our social and political life. We can also assume it is only beginning. While television itself is being transformed via satellite, cable, laser, computer, video tape, video disc and other developments, the upheaval is bound to dislocate further the world of the printed word, and the roles it has played.

READING, TELEVISION AND ACCULTURATION

One reason for this deep impact is so obvious that it is seldom mentioned or discussed. Reading is an acquired skill mastered with effort—and usually with much guidance—over a span of years. Television viewing calls for no skill, beyond normal human functions. Viewing can begin in cradle or playpen and often does.

Consider the implications. A child's introduction to the printed word is a gradual process that has traditionally been helped and guided by father, mother, grandfather, grandmother, sister, brother, teacher, clergyman. From reading aloud it has gone on to intensive drill, trial and error and—usually—a degree of mastery and enjoyment. The process itself has favored social continuity, a transmittal of values, attitudes, beliefs. The printed word, which in its early history had a revolutionary effect on society, began ultimately to serve, in the main, a stabilizing social function.

Now, with television, the process has been short-circuited. Television can commuciate with a new human being directly, bypassing mother, father, grandparent and all the other home-based mediating influences. They have largely lost this role in the socializing process. Noting the child's absorption in the tube, they have tended to surrender the role readily, without glimpsing possible long-range consequences.

In cradle or playpen, the child sees across the room a bright oblong—the brightest thing in the home. Its colors are more splendid than anything else in sight. Dazzling figures move about in it; challenging sounds emerge from it. These are in time sensed as belonging to a world outside the home. The figures and actions begin to define what that world is like, and how its people behave toward one another. Gradually the child discerns that some things and people are considered evil and others good. A pattern of assumptions and beliefs begins to take shape.

Television gets to the child years before teacher and clergyman, age-old promulgators of group heritage and values, and years before the printed words and images over which they preside. All these may add only footnotes to the child's emerging picture of the larger world and his or her expectations for activity in it.

What this means is not only that the role of print has changed, but that the shift has rearranged the acculturation process, with effects that may already be comparable to those involved in the advent of print. When we consider the ramifications of the new television-related technologies, it seems likely that the resulting social and political upheavals will be on a larger scale.

WHO CONTROLS THE TUBE?

To assess the possible impact, we should first note that the pre-television leaders in the acculturation process—family, teacher and so on—have not been able to control the ideas and images on the tube. They have occasionally, belatedly, struggled to control them but have largely failed; at least, they have failed in the United States and in societies most influenced by it. Control of the tube has gone to the world of business, for purposes of merchandising, public relations and political persuasion. In a development without precedent, their messages have become our dominant social doctrines.

The messages are spearheaded, of course, by "commercials" (of various kinds from product advertising to political propaganda) clustered in and around our programs. The messages, multiplying until they are now spread through all hours of day and night, stress a consumption-dominated life and the successes in business and personal relations that are to flow from it. An increasing number of commercials also address the political concerns of sponsors. The funds expended on production of the messages far exceed, on a per-minute basis, the funds lavished on intervening programs. The messages are the main focus of sponsor attention, and earn for the acting profession more than all theatrical films and television program performances combined.

The sponsors say they do not wish to control the programs in which the messages are placed, but in effect they do. Since a sponsor is often ready to pay premium prices (at times, hundreds of thousands of dollars for a single 30-second network spot) for positions in programs that seem certain to reach his target audience, the quest for programs meeting this objective dominates network thinking. The demographic formulas of our entertainment programs—characters, settings, techniques, themes, myths—reflect this feverish quest. The meagerness of time devoted to documentary and news programs, and the zealous efforts to infuse them with patterns connoting "entertainment," reflect it further. Most of our program schedule, in style and content, is an emanation of our sponsorship system, in which "market forces" have been allowed free rein.

Political Impact

It should be noted that this system has in a number of ways scrambled our political system, giving it a character distinct from systems of most leading nations. In most other countries, time for campaign debates between major candidates is by law allocated to parties free of charge, in proportion to registered party membership, membership in a legislature or votes in a previous election. In the United States, the stratospheric market value of television time—plus *laissez-faire* regulatory practices—have prompted networks and stations to decline allotment on any such basis, except for a rare superstar presidential debate. Candidates for major office find they must approach television as sponsors, buying short time segments at fantastic commercial rates; the resulting "commercials" (candidates themselves use the term) are often produced and placed by the same advertising agencies merchandising products.

The election process has thus been virtually integrated into the merchandising world. It has happened so gradually that it has been taken for granted. Meanwhile the rising cost of the procedure has made fund-raising a nightmare concern for candidates. They have become crucially dependent on funds provided by PACs—political action committees—among which the PACs sponsored by business organizations have become the most affluent. Candidates who, by their records or commitments, can win the contributions of such PACs for their television campaigns, have been increasingly successful in capturing elections. Thus again, business influence reaches beyond business practice into our political fabric. The days when a "stump speech" could be delivered from a tree stump, and its wider dissemination was the work of print media, are long gone.

That religions have experienced a similar scrambling, favoring aggressive television salesmanship in paid-for time, has been widely noted.

Public Acceptance

Whatever objections have been raised by individuals and groups, there seems no question that the commercial evolution of American television has proceeded with wide public acceptance. Year by year American television has held and generally increased its hold on audiences. Time-sale revenues continue to rise. A long-time National Association of Broadcasters president, Vincent T. Wasilewski, called American television "the most successful and universally accepted business enterprise in history," and there is little basis for disputing him. By making time, i.e., public attention, a for-sale commodity at free-market rates and permitting the buying and selling of channels with minimal regulation, television has brought business to its present commanding position. And business-oriented television has, as *Advertising Age* puts it, "revolutionized everything from sales pitches to politics." [1]

Protests from educators, environmentalists and others appear to have had little effect on audience fidelity. So steady has this been that few major corporations dare to be absent from the roster of sponsors. As underwriters they also have an increasing voice in so-called noncommercial ("public") television, in which program proposals must often await corporate funding to reach production. Here, too, business has become a powerful, though less overt, force.

---

1. "Advertising: 1776-1976," *Advertising Age*, April 19, 1976.

Impact Abroad

More important in global terms is the fact that American programs, particularly those made for commercial network sponsorship, reach into more than a hundred other countries, dominating the systems of many. Since production costs have generally been amortized via sponsorship on American television, most foreign systems can buy the programs at a small fraction of the cost of producing such programs themselves. This makes the programs highly marketable for sponsorship abroad, often by foreign corporations affiliated with American corporations. Thus the programming continues to exert, throughout much of the world, influences paralleling those in the United States. American television is a worldwide acculturation agency.

EFFECT ON PRINT PUBLICATIONS

Considering the extraordinary dominance of television, here and abroad, the continuing high level of activity in the world of print is perhaps surprising. In spite of predictions, the reader is not a dying species. It is true that "reading readiness" among those entering school seems to have suffered from television addiction, and functional illiterates are numerous even among those with years of schooling—a problem generally felt to be related to television. Yet at the same time, books are printed in millions of copies, magazine racks are crammed with periodicals old and new, many libraries hum with activity, and newspapers, though diminishing in numbers, show no signs of disappearing as an institution. What we are witnessing seems less a collapse than a series of shifts in function and content. In various ways, the shifts seem related to the dominance of television.

Periodicals

Numerous magazines prosper by exploring private lives of stars seen on television and of a huge miscellany of celebrities—

well-known "for their well-knownness," as Daniel Boorstin has put it—that parade through quiz, game and talk shows. Another group of magazines, profusely illustrated, recycles story lines of daytime serials. One of the most successful of all magazines, *TV Guide*, specializes in the dissemination of television schedules and program information. Comparable services have apparently become a life-or-death matter for many newspapers.

While many periodicals have thus become satellites of television, still others survive and even thrive by offering material that our television has generally not wished or dared to provide. Magazines portraying nudity and sexual activity are an example. Other examples are the innumerable special-interest informational magazines. Particularly important to the democratic process are the magazines belonging to the literature of dissent which probe and agitate issues that a business-oriented television prefers to ignore, or to present in neat capsules drained of meaning.

Books

Segments of the book industry likewise derive importance from positions outside television. Reference and information functions — except for merchandising purposes — have so far hardly been touched by television, although a few experiments, including an online encyclopedia, are under way and other computer-related services are likely to emerge.

As a dissent and debate channel the book publishing industry, because of the rise of television, has become crucially important, serving diverse interests and functions. One of these, not surprisingly, is the assessment and criticism of American television as a bulwark of oligopoly. Such books, unfortunately, reach only the well-functioning reader, and rising book prices may become a barrier to wide readership (although unit books sales are flat, not declining, and an explosion in the number of bookstores in the past 10 years has made books more widely available than ever before).

A major segment of the book industry, publishers of mass market paperbacks, sells its wares in drugstores and super- markets as well as bookstores. Many of these books—still low in cost by comparison with other forms of entertainment —echo television. Such books constantly recycle fiction that has been successful in television adaptations and present new fiction designed for similar recycling. A new novel may now find its greatest success when it becomes a popular theatrical motion picture that is then shown on television, then re- processed as a television series or mini-series, and eventually returned to book racks as an illustrated paperback in a "television edition." Much of the book industry dances around the television maypole.

Are the Buyers Reading?

The burgeoning role of illustrations in today's books and magazines poses questions. Are these publications *read*, or do people buy them to look at pictures? Is the text included mainly to give the work reading-matter status? Or, under the growing influence of visual media, are we returning to a pre-print state in which images and rituals served as basic media of communication, providing a largely illiterate public with its main cohesive myths and ideas? This is the thesis suggested by Gregor T. Goethals in *The TV Ritual*.

SCIENTIFIC INQUIRY VS. SPECULATION

Much research on the social and psychological effects of television has used scientific procedures, in which answers to thousands of questions are fed into computers, and charts based on the data are compiled. It is doubtful whether such approaches can really illuminate these matters. Control groups are not available: we live under the shadow of television whether or not we watch it. And the answers that people give about media behavior and motives for it, to questions designed to provide the "quantitative" data congenial to computerized research, are likely to be convenient evasions of complex actualities. The choices we make stem from numerous levels of the conscious and unconscious, and computer-oriented questions are more than likely to produce simplistic answers.

If the recent past and present are thus shrouded in mysteries, the future is even more unknowable through scientific inquiry. Yet it is surely a topic for piquant speculation. The new television-related media have become prime topics for such speculation.

Each major medium introduced in the 19th and 20th centuries—the photograph, telegraph, telephone, phonograph, wireless, radio, frequency modulation, television—was greeted with sweeping predictions, some doom-laden but in most cases euphoric. Possible blessings are easier to glimpse than problems, and are more pleasant to contemplate. And they stimulate investment and enterprise. Each new medium was thus depicted as leading to a more richly informed and educated public, and the fulfillment of democracy. All this is true of the spate of new television-related inventions.

Let us summarize prevailing scenarios. They are not science fiction: the needed technologies exist and in some cases are being applied, if only to a limited extent. They largely await the formation of business and governmental alignments and commitments that will make their full implementation feasible.

THE HOME/OFFICE COMMUNICATION CENTER

The television set in your home or office becomes a kind of computerized communication center. It has two-way capability. The picture tube or screen is supplemented by a printout facility. To the screen, via numerous pushbuttons, you can summon television programs of the sort long available —drama, sports, documentaries, variety programs, newscasts, cultural events — but also numerous other choices: films or documents from diverse data banks, some requiring the use of codes; tapes or video discs from your private collection, including games, memorabilia or your own video creations; items in a department store, which you can order by pushbutton. You can also call up pre-packaged lectures in a college course, which you can take for credit. Pursuing such a course on your own timetable, you summon the exam when you feel ready; its questions appear on your screen, to be answered by pushbutton. Your grade is automatically recorded in a data bank; you get a file copy by pushing your printout button.

Some of the items summoned to your screen and/or ordered by pushbutton come free, while others involve a fee. The same applies to printouts requested via your printout button. The screen keeps warning you when you are about to enter a payment area. Payment is procedurally simple: as you confirm your order, a deduction is made simultaneously from your computerized bank account.

The two-way feature of your communication center involves not only pushbutton feedback arrangements but a microphone and camera. They allow much business to be conducted by television. A company's executives in six cities—each person in his own office—hold a conference via the video screen. Each sees the others simultaneously on a split screen: this permits very concentrated face-to-face negotiation. Much business can also be conducted from the home, with data and documents supplied via screen and printout. As futurists put it, "message movement" replaces "people movement." They see the process ending the madness of rush-hour traffic.

Postal authorities have similar dreams of ending their particular chaos. Electronic letters addressed to you are displayed on your screen; if you want a permanent copy, you push your printout button. Newspapers, public notices, advertisements, can be delivered the same way. So can tax forms, unless taxes become an automatic computerized deduction with every transaction, scarcely noticed. At election time your ballot appears on the screen and you vote by pushbutton; again "people movement" is avoided. Futurists see all this as helping to solve the energy crisis.

Meanwhile doctors take up "telemedicine." Some make home visits by two-way television, surveying your symptoms via audio and video, sometimes with help from a visiting nurse. And a Spokane surgeon performing an operation on a visitor from Paris can summon relevant medical records and charts from abroad to a hospital video screen.

Much that reaches your screen comes via a strand of glass fibre the thickness of a human hair, propelled by a laser beam that flows through it. This fibre has such an extraordinary message-carrying capacity that it can carry, in both directions, all needed video, voice and computer signals. They all become part of one system. Your television screen is your two-way telephone screen, bulletin board, education blackboard, ballot box, lectern, shopping plaza, family game screen, recipe file. You may need one in every room.

NEW TECHNOLOGIES AND THE DEMOCRATIC IDEAL

Will all this bring the well-informed public, the fulfillment of democracy?

Gatekeepers, Old and New

It seems useful, at this point, to look back at the advent of print from movable type, and the nature of its social impact. The emergence of printing is said to have ended a long era during which the church, holding a virtual communication monopoly, presided over the distribution of knowledge and ideas. The monopoly was based on the scarcity of parchment and the skills of monastery copyists. Their labors kept ancient knowledge and wisdom in circulation, and provided material for the education of new scholars. But what they kept in circulation was carefully selected and controlled by the gatekeepers of the era, the church.

The monopoly held so long as parchment, a scarce item, was an essential part of the process. But paper and techniques for making it began arriving from the east, and when the possibility existed of making paper cheaply and in quantity, the monopoly was undermined. Now it became logical to make printing presses, which had always been possible but hardly made sense until paper was plentiful. Presses and paper: now the gatekeepers could be bypassed. New knowledge and opinion, fact and fiction, began to flow out into the world, and became a swelling tide. Independent voices were heard. Ideas never transmitted via establishment copyists — including ideas considered heretical—went into wide circulation. Reasons to learn to read multiplied. The reverberations were extraordinary. He who introduced print with movable type, wrote Thomas Carlyle, "was disbanding hired armies, and cashiering most Kings and Senates, and creating a whole new democratic world." [2]

But of course this new technology, while upsetting an old monopoly, also offered opportunities for new monopolies. In England, under Henry VIII and others, the press led to a licensing system. The operation of a printing press required a special royal license. To communicate with the public through this powerful new medium one had to be royally approved or deal with those who had been given licenses, and whose position of royal privilege made them cautious and tended to seal their loyaly. Gatekeepers of a new sort, serving the royal gatekeeper, took their position in society.

The long struggles against this system, including John Milton's eloquent *Areopagitica*—published without the seal of approval — are familiar history. Rulers acted "injuriously," wrote Milton, when they sought to stifle "the winds of doctrine" by a license requirement. Freedom from licensing became a *cause célèbre* of generations. When our founding fathers in the Bill of Rights spoke of freedom of the press, they

2. *Sartor Resartus*, chapter 5.

meant precisely *freedom from licensing*. They were resolved that in this new nation, no one would need government permission to communicate with the public.

It is ironic that when broadcasting began, soon producing periods of spectrum chaos, a licensing system seemed an inescapable engineering necessity to make the medium workable. Lawmakers writing our broadcasting legislation were conscious of the irony, and therefore proclaimed that commissions regulating the spectrum must not censor. But this did not alter the basic troublesome fact: radio and television, the media that have dominated the past half century, have had as their foundation the very thing our founding fathers were determined to prevent. To communicate with the public through these media has required a federal license, or dealings with the limited number who had one, and whose privileged position tended to overlay every decision.

The no-censorship dictum hardly solved the problem; if anything, it has strengthened the monopolistic position of the new gatekeepers — the licensees and the buyers of time whose funds won dominance of the system. For those outside the system, it has meant a constant, and usually futile, probing for "access."

We have now arrived at a thought-provoking juncture in this history. A cluster of new technologies seems to threaten the structure we have known. Will they bring a new day for independent voices, an opportunity to bypass established gatekeepers, as did the printing press centuries ago? While many argue that they will, voices of dissent and even alarm are also sounded.

Interactive Television

To true believers in the new technologies, the advent of two-way "interactive" television represents an extraordinary democratic breakthrough, one which will finally give *vox populi* its due role in the scheme of things. To others the

privilege of pushbutton participation is almost a mockery of
the idea of democracy. It completes the process of reducing
political discourse to pollster formulations. And the microphone and camera as key elements in the home or office
system, playing a role in business dealings, private con-
versations, health services, credit inquiries and other matters,
would seem to pose grave dangers to privacy.

Some of the blessings most enthusiastically advertised by
existing two-way cable experiments, such as burglary protection (in your absence, your camera can monitor your
premises, and any intruder can be videotaped) provide the
basic elements of a surveillance system. There is also the
consideration that whatever goes out from your communication center, via pushbutton or microphone or camera,
can be recorded and stored elsewhere. In the process, an
astonishing amount of private information about anyone can
be stored in data banks. No matter how well protected by
coded-access devices, privacy is seen by some doubters as the
price we shall pay for the blessings of the new technology. This
is a warning sharply sounded by John Wicklein in *Electronic
Nightmare: The New Technology and Freedom*. It is likewise
the message of George Orwell's *1984*.

Optical Fibre

To enthusiasts, optical fibre with its promise of hundreds of
choices for the home viewer — a multiplicity far exceeding
that offered by present cable systems — spells unprecedented
enrichment of our lives. Others argue that multiplicity does
not assure diversity, and never has. What gatekeepers will
control the fibre channels, with what objectives in mind?
AT&T, a leader in the fibre development, is the company that
guided the strategy under which our broadcasting system
came to be devoted primarily to business interests. And since
all services to your home screen—and your electronic re-
sponses to them—can flow through one fibre connection,

some see the possibilities for centralized control as strengthened, to a degree without precedent.

Communication Satellites

To some, the advent of communication satellites, making distance meaningless and theoretically putting the world at your fingertips, means another momentous enrichment. And obviously such enrichment is possible. But the satellites—an invention which, like radio, was largely developed at public expense and then transferred to private enterprise—are controlled by the companies dominating our present communication arrangements; they include, among others, AT&T, General Electric, Westinghouse, IT&T and Western Union International, all familiar names in communication history. Whatever changes and new developments may come to pass, there apparently will be no great shuffling of gatekeepers—or of priorities.

Personal Computers

To enthusiasts, the incorporation of the computer terminal into a home or office communication center, providing the possibility of access to diverse data banks throughout the world, means another source of enrichment. But others, noting that this development is inextricably involved with business interests, see it as a guarantee of increasing business dominance. It is also linked to the privacy hazard.

The Video Disc

To many, the video disc offers extraordinary possibilities. It would seem to be the ultimate medium for a private collection of classics or for a public archive: durable, compact, noise-free. The laser-read disc creates the possibility of storing all the pictures in the Louvre on one video disc. For the preservation and circulation of the world's cultural heritage, this invention would seem preeminent. But again, it involves high costs and a complex technology firmly controlled by current gatekeepers. It does not seem likely to put new or dissident ideas into circulation.

VIDEO AS A CREATIVE MEDIUM

Most aspects of the new technology are concerned with the storage and distribution rather than the creative use of media. All involve gatekeepers, who appear to be the present gatekeepers. Most seem more likely to strengthen than to weaken present controls.

If there is a wild card in the deck, with a possibility of leading in a contrary direction, it is probably *video* — video tape used as a medium of expression. Its significance is complex, with ramifications that link it with the world of print.

Video tape recorders came on the market in the 1950s, with prices ranging upward from $40,000. They at once gave television networks an improved means for recording live television programs and rebroadcasting them. Video tape thus promptly supplanted the generally unsatisfactory kinescope, a film made by focusing a film camera on a television tube during a performance. As video tape recorders dropped sharply in price, and the advent of cassettes made them easier to operate, recorders began to be used in home and school for keeping copies of broadcast programs. This was seen as a threat to copyright owners, film distributors and the incipient video disc industry. Major elements in the entertainment industry became ambivalent about video tape, seeking alternately to utilize it, control it and block its advances.

Meanwhile the introduction of video tape cameras, increasingly compact and portable, brought the medium into a new arena, associated with the word *video*. As a means for creating an original work, not merely recording and recycling a Hollywood offering, video was seen to have unique character-

istics. As equipment prices continued to drop, these characteristics began to have revolutionary implications. A wide range
of individuals and groups began to involve themselves in video
production.

New Freedom for Producers

By eliminating laboratory processing, video offered the
producer a freedom from uncertainties, delays and costs
inherent in film production, whether in 35mm, 16mm or 8mm.
Images could be seen and evaluated instantly, and reshot if
unsatisfactory. Not only did this speed production and
eliminate costs: it gave new zest and spontaneity—a freedom
from anxiety—to the production process. Independents working alone or with small units felt these blessings even more
intensely than the Hollywood producer, whose proceedings
were necessarily rigidified by unions and guilds, and the
resulting size of production units. Meanwhile the development
of electronic editing equipment speeded the editing process
and offered magical new advantages for special effects of
diverse kinds. Even independents working in their homes
began to use computers for the processing of images and for
computerized animation.

A Teaching/Training Tool

In schools the impact of the new advantages was especially
resounding. Teachers found that even elementary school
children could use video equipment with little inhibition, and
its use yielded new adventures in discovery. The child could
suddenly see himself as others saw him; he could see himself in
action in relation to others. This means of self-revelation was
also of interest to psychiatrists, who began to record interview
sessions for later review with patients. For training of all
kinds, video was quickly recognized as the most effective tool
ever invented. Again and again, a pupil could review his

own performance, modifying it step by step. This was equally applicable in musical performance, machine shop operations, sports, military maneuvers and sales techniques.

Community Impact

Video began to play a varied role in the community. An increasing awareness of community activities and problems was the first gain. The public-access channels in most cable systems sparked little interest and had minimal impact when they were used only for speeches and panel discussions from a studio. When groups took up video production, documenting in the field the problems that concerned them, the access channels acquired a dimension of their own.

In New York a group of Chinese began to give New Yorkers glimpses of life in Chinatown unlike anything they had seen before. Another group documented, with chilling impact, some of the problems in a local hospital. Pollution violations were documented.

A remarkable aspect of such activities was that the traditional gap between "professional" and "semiprofessional" or "amateur" images was suddenly vanishing. The documentary sequences shot by Jon Alpert for New York's Downtown Community Television Center, on a host of topics, were so extraordinary that network television began to negotiate for their use and to emulate Alpert's methods. Material taped for projects of limited purpose — a group therapy session, a tenant meeting planning a rent strike, a sports training session, a music lesson — were found to have fascination far beyond the original function, and sometimes received use in new contexts. Video was thus full of serendipity. And the wall between an entertainment "industry" and entertainment "consumers" was starting to crumble. Americans were becoming their own entertainment industry, or an important segment of it.

An Explosion of Activity

In 1981 a first National Video Festival, organized by the American Film Institute, was held in Washington. It featured hundreds of works made during the first decade of video by a huge range of individuals, groups, schools and companies, for an equally huge range of purposes. The occasion was a revelation to many who attended. An enormous ferment was obviously at work.

The exhibits ranged from documentary material to imaginative fiction. They included animation made by computer. They included biting satire. They included works done by the very young and the very old. Much of the work made a strong impact.

One of the significant points behind all this activity was that the basic material, video tape, had reached a price level at which an individual artist or group could contemplate using it freely, as an author uses paper, with little inhibition stemming from its cost. Used tape could even be reused.

At the same time the basic equipment, the video camera, had reached a price level comparable to that of a good typewriter. Ownership was not limited to companies or rich individuals. A video camera could be put into the hands of a child.

And the independent creator, being freed from dependence on processing laboratories and the costs and delays involved, had an increasing sense of independence. A lone individual could be a complete production unit.

VIDEO AS A DELIVERY SYSTEM

Unlike satellite, cable, fibre and video disc, the video tape was not merely a distribution mechanism but a medium of expression. Yet it was also a delivery system.

Ultimately addressing its audience through television screens already in place in hundreds of millions of locations, video tape had many routes for reaching those screens. It could do so through our television networks, but it could also bypass them. It could feed into cable and fibre networks but also bypass them. It could reach out through satellites but need not. It could be mass-duplicated and marketed like a book via stores, organizations or mail order.

The book analogy is fitting in a number of ways. The ½-inch cassette is comparable in size to a paperback, fits neatly on shelves like a book, is comparable in price to a book. It can be marketed via sale and / or rental. Means for using it are widely available in home, office, school, museum, library, church, community center, hotel room, party headquarters, factory.

The cassette player is becoming one of the most prevalent of utilities. Use requires no technical skill or training. As a basis for group discussion video offers advantages never achieved by print. A video work can be readily marketed in small or large editions, and can therefore give economical service to specialized groups

All this has meaning for the scholar, artist, teacher, politician, doctor, businessman, organizer, salesman, diplomat, coach. In short, it has implications for countless pursuits involving education, persuasion, documentation or inspiration. As a medium of artistic expression video has won a place in leading museums. As a communication medium in the broadest sense it is winning a place in libraries. At the Library of Congress new facilities for the study of video tapes have been designed with multiple uses in mind. A central aspect of the plan is that a research scholar (historian, scientist, sociologist, anthropologist, media specialist, artist or whatever) should be able in a sound-proof booth, equipped with video monitor and speaker, to do his viewing without actual possession of the tape. It can be fed to him via cable by a technician in the storage area. At the same time the researcher —if the feed is from a video cassette—can through a remote control mechanism be given the capability to stop, start, reverse and freeze frame. In terms of security and the preservation of valuable holdings, such possibilities have important implications for libraries.

Video serves the democratic process by making possible access to the home screen without the blessing of the gatekeepers that have dominated television during its first decades. This aspect links it with the segment of the print world already playing a crucial role in political discussion and dissent. At the same time, video has the advantage of conveying meaning to many for whom the printed page has become a foreign land. Together, print and video may offer our best hope for revitalizing the democratic process.

THE UNPREDICTABLE FUTURE

Will it happen—and happen in this way? Who can tell? Every scenario holds countless pitfalls. Some involve psychological factors hardly considered by the scenarists. Most prognostications seem to come from people who love gadgets better than people. They call for people to sit at home watching their screens, manipulating pushbuttons and sometimes talking to images on their screens. Experiences of this sort are to take the place of visits to stores, campuses, polling booths, churches, banks, offices, clinics and other locations. We are to be saved from people movement. This is described as practical, convenient and even good. Its convenience is somewhat like that of having hens spend their lives in egg-laying cubicles. Is it the good life? Have the scenarists any notion of the mass malaise they may be hatching with their plans?

There are countless other uncertainties. In the background, as we speculate with agreeable detachment, there is a rumble of widespread corporate struggles in which territories are being staked out. There is little public knowledge of the stakes in those struggles. Beyond the corporate wars are international struggles. Control of markets and control of raw materials are the ultimate concern of multinational corporations that have dominated our communication channels, and of the political forces that have dominated communication systems in other countries. Communication satellites, ours and theirs, and the possibility that they will beam messages (including news, drama, quiz and game shows, sports, special events) directly to rooftop dishes across distant borders, will bring the rivalries into unprecedented collision.

The television image, and the video media that create that image, may be part of this turmoil, with all its potential for good and evil. Whatever video ultimately turns out to be, it will certainly be far more than the "entertainment" people once thought it was.

3

Authors Versus Books

by Anthony Smith

The system of moving letters devised by Johan Gutenberg established, or rather confirmed, a chain of specialist relationships which runs: author, printer, bookseller/publisher, reader, librarian. For five centuries these have been the principal actors in the politics of the text; they have fought one another and depended upon one another; they have been held together (or apart) by a body of law and professional doctrine. Printer, bookseller/publisher and their ancillary crafts and trades were all once firmly held within the Stationers' Company, but as the printing press technology spread beyond guild control in the late 17th century these functions diverged more and more.

We inherit the rituals and procedures of these separate professional groups and their relative status. They have seemed to us as inevitable as the seasons and as essentially *separate*. Not even those revolutionary prophets of the early 20th century who predicted the withering away of the state considered that a technology might arrive, as suddenly but as profoundly needed as the printing press, which would lead us to question the settled assumptions of the Renaissance. For that is what the new technology of the text—a technology consisting of computers, telecommunications and display devices—urges us to do: at least, to dig out some of the unargued assumptions about the nature of authorship, say, compared with librarianship, about the relationship also between publisher and librarian, and so forth.

THE CONCEPT OF AUTHORSHIP

The development of this technology is not the only phenomenon which is causing us to reconsider the nature of the author. The other collective cultural processes of the century (cinema, television especially) have all had to confront the problem of the author. Students of cinema were the first to enquire where the "author" lay in a film, since our culture predisposes us to believe instinctively that authorship must lie somewhere at the heart of every text. The debate over the "auteur" has now vexed two generations of film studies and continues to divide the critics into those who believe the director is a (kind of) author and those who believe something else. The rival doctrines have of course exercised a profound influence over the kinds of films that are made—especially those made by critics, as in France in the 1950s and 1960s. Certainly, a kind of Heisenbergian syndrome has operated in this area, so that the very question of whether a film is made by an auteur forces the next film selfconsciously to betray the spores of the argument and so confuse it further.

We habitually use the name of an author to identify portmanteaus of data and indeed to give a certain authority to whole areas of discourse or to particular perspectives on them. We speak of Marx or Milton Friedman or John Kenneth Galbraith; we use the terms Picasso, Schoenberg or D.W. Griffith to designate blocks of cultural experience. We permit penumbral meanings to be associated with historical personages who are often in no way responsible for or even connected with the phenomena which they are taken to qualify: we refer to Dickensian conditions, Cartesian ideas, Rabelaisian wit.

Post-Renaissance, post-Gutenbergian civilization is heavily oriented toward authors. We store our information and teach outlines of our societies' history in terms of individuals to an extent that is not really borne out by experience. An author is often merely a point in a continuum of creativity, the re-maker rather than the maker of a myth, a member of a school the other members of which may be neglected or forgotten. We recognize the importance of "borrowings" from writer to writer, and in the visual field from director to director, but without removing the author from the central niche. "The dead authors are what we are," argued T.S. Eliot.

Both in the field of written literature and of the moving image we have begun to question the easy assumption that a text is the primary moral property and spiritual emanation of an author. We have started to demystify authorship, at least to the extent of stripping away the uninvited 19th century individualism which has recently shrouded it. Perhaps the new text technologies, which so profoundly change the nature of information, will further undermine the accepted inherited ideas concerning the constitution of the author and the nature of the book.

THE DISTURBING FORCE OF INNOVATION

We are told by Plato that when writing itself was offered by its inventor to the King of Thebes, it was rejected by him on the grounds that it would destroy memory. It was a disorganizing force, insidious to the prevailing system for storing and communicating information. It created new cadres of specialists on whom the rest of society had henceforth to depend, as we have done on television producers for our political information, or on record companies for our music. Indeed, every new communications system that has ever come into being has had the effect of restructuring and displacing, usurping the settled functions of established institutions, disturbing religious beliefs and undermining the credibility of rituals. It is disturbing to live through an age in which the dominant information mode is being replaced. But that is where we are today.

An age of change is also an age of improvisation. It's a moment when principles become insecure. There appear to be about half a dozen distinct ways in which the computerization of information is transforming basic underlying principles which entered our society at the time of the Gutenbergian revolution, or even before it. If one considers them separately and then aggregates them it is possible to see more clearly, though still in a cloudy crystal ball, how the concept of the author may be giving some ground to a newer post-Gutenbergian principle, of which we today can envisage only the merest shadow.

THE SHRINKING WORLD

First, distance is rapidly disappearing as a factor in the cost of transporting text. Broadband communication highways, involving satellites, coaxial cables and optic fibres all in interconnection are now quite rapidly reducing the distance element as a factor in calculating the total cost of an information transaction. Thus, we may send words and figures from continent to continent as cheaply, or almost as cheaply, as from street to street. Gradually these broadband systems are spreading from the major highways to the more local routes and eventually, if not already, will bring text (as well as speech and moving image) directly to our home or automobile with the same relative disregard for the distance of the communication. This is not the result of a single technology but of a whole series of new technologies and the efforts of the institutions that operate them to exploit them as efficaciously and profitably as possible.

The same, of course, applies to information which is held in computer storage or in digital form. Great blocks of data move about the globe awaiting use in whatever section of a network has parking room at a given moment. It is as hard to argue "that's my data" as it is to look at the balance sheet of a bank and say "that's my money." Both cash and data are subject to electronic storage and lose physical existence until they reappear again in physical words printed via a piece of terminal equipment, or as specie handed out in a bank. Digital data is essentially placeless, whether it's the airways timetable or Saul Bellow's new novel waiting to drive a printing press.

GROWTH AND DECLINE
OF THE GUTENBERGIAN PRINCIPLE

The second changing principle is the Gutenbergian principle itself—the notion that the audience is reached by multiplying the physical number of copies of a text until the number equates with the number of people who can be identified as requiring the information. This idea is so obvious to us today that it's invisible. We live surrounded by the institutional implications of the idea, and yet it has become an extremely inconvenient one, an idea whose time has gone, rather than come. One should compare the condition of literature after Gutenberg with the condition before he invented moving letters.

From Preservation to Originality

In the age of the manuscript the central problem of the intellectual, so to speak, was to see to the preservation of knowledge through the care of the physical text. The accumulation of knowledge was essentially a race against time. Kronos was the enemy of information since he saw to it that the physical materials which held it self-destructed more rapidly than the copyists could reproduce it. Only the most solid of materials—from granite to vellum—could be relied upon.

When paper reached Europe in the 10th century, it was deliberately "de-invented" and not encouraged greatly until the age of printing, since it flaked away far too quickly to enable important information to survive. Treaties and charters, for example, could not be trusted to this ephemeral substance. The guardian or custodian of a celebrated manuscript was as crucial a figure as its author. Texts became in some cases sacral objects in themselves, more sacral than their authors. The copyists were an industry whose chief functions were to defeat time, to purify the text of previous error, to check the text against other surviving versions. The intellectual moved towards the text not vice versa.

However, the technique of moving letters transformed the entire culture of the text and all the beliefs and assumptions which belonged to the manuscript era. Information could suddenly burst the bonds of time and of space, through the power of multiplication.

Within a few decades the entire decomposing body of ancient texts was reproduced in printed form, transported to hundreds of centers. Erasmus proclaimed the "library without walls," i.e., the phenomenon of infinite reproducibility of *identical* text. The Gutenbergian principle transformed the prevailing concept of knowledge itself, making it subject to constant augmentation through addition, comparison and controversy rather than subject to an overriding need for recovery and preservation.

Knowledge was now felt to be something one did not but might have, rather than something which had been lost but might be found again. Knowledge exists somewhere between now and the future, and we reach it by way of *authors* who sit at the center of the text—apparently—who guarantee the text through the application of their names to it, who augment knowledge through the dextrous use of intellect and memory, playing upon the growing corpus of aggregative text.

The author was slowly separated from the tradition and treated as an exogenous phenomenon, an individual mind playing upon the body of human perception. The inventor was treated in a similar way, as a semi-sacral figure whose innovative impulses were deemed to be more important than his aggregative functions. Originality became the most highly prized of qualities in post-Renaissance culture and only through originality did information turn into property as it passed through the mysterious but duplicative processes of the printing house.

As the text multiplied it spread the author through time and space; it inflated him as the originating subject. The new legal systems began their new fascination with this more abstract form of property, information, which was henceforth subject both to organized censorship and organized protection, for it generated both fresh uncontrollable political power and fresh uncontrollable capital. Around the author sat publisher, printer, bookseller, all juridically dependent upon this intellectual apparatus, all bent upon exploiting it but defining their economic circumstances through the support of the author and the glorification of the author.

An Exhausted Form

It is this system, which we may call the Gutenbergian, that is now coming to an end, at least in certain crucial respects. In information overload the system begins to meet its own internal contradictions. The principle, we begin to discover in the second half of the 20th century, functions efficiently only at a certain size of market and at a certain level of costs. The book, as a form, no longer works for all the categories of information which we cherish and, as a form, it is clearly attempting to perform functions which are beyond it.

Let us take—only partly humorously—the example of the telephone directory which is a compendium of small nuggets of information only one or two of which are required by a given reader during the entire active lifetime of the text. It becomes increasingly expensive to accumulate, reproduce and distribute the information within the time of validity of the information itself. Its value has begun to erode the moment the ink is applied to the paper, or even before. And yet until now the telephone directory has operated within the Gutenbergian mode, the number of copies growing with the number of anticipated users.

The idea has simply exhausted itself and is crying out for a return to the manuscript mode, the single copy of valid information from which the individual reader merely extracts the pieces of information which are required. Computer storage is clearly the only means by which the contradiction can be resolved. It is only a question of time—very little time—before the cost of the alternative mode drops below the rising costs of the exhausted mode.

When one looks at the various collections of information contained in a modern library, one can perceive many that are comparable to the telephone directory, including many which appear to be "authored" works. Indeed, much academic research consists of the running together of contemporary pieces of scholarship which are made to take the form of printed papers or printed books. Intellectual work has to be performed in the process, of course, but it is really the work of the collator, or organizer, or analyst, rather akin to a kind of microlibrarianship.

THE ROLE OF GOVERNMENT

The third and fourth principles need to be laid out side by side in order to explain them. Government is having to play a more central role in the new text technologies than in the traditional one. However, government is ceasing to play a role in the organization of audiences. Of course, governments have always been involved in directing the information flows of society. From the moment that Socrates describes when written text began "to pass into the hands of people who have no business with it" it was clear that a text has a life of its own, separate from that of its author; it has many meanings and implications for many people.

Controlling the Flow of Information

All governments make laws that lay down certain boundaries for certain types of statement, even those governments based on 18th century constitutions proclaiming rights of free expression and press freedom. Governments took some time to develop the idea that the more closely involved authority is with a given piece of information, the less credence it commands. There have been societies in which a quite contrary belief was held—there still are.

For the most part, governments take the path of caution and insist on controlling the industries of publishing and of education. However, there exist a few societies today, a small minority of the total, who choose to assert the separation of government from information as a matter of high principle, although even these tend to overlook the areas of continuing government involvement.

A developing society faces a much more serious contradiction than an already developed one, since the former is having constantly to assert its own existence economically and politically, to press the world to see it as an independent entity so that it can become an independent entity. Thus, in the Third World, it is almost impossible for a government to open up the sphere of information to competition; only through control does it retain the semblance of its political integrity, even though that control undermines the intellectual development of the society itself.

Developed societies, however, enjoy a much greater possibility of riding this contradiction. The United States provides an example of an extreme version of the free information principle, but today confronts the new age of text technology which is forcing it to reconsider the whole range of censorship issues. All of the new apparatus depends upon telecommunications and upon the controlling, reorganizing or dismantling of great areas of industry which make, maintain and distribute the equipment that enables the new systems of information transfer.

Government finds itself having either to legislate or to arbitrate between conflicting interests and principles. It has to determine what privacy means in the context of the new technologies, what constitutes a monopoly, how far a powerful controller of blocks of data should be permitted to monopolize the manipulation or processing of the resulting blocks of text. True, censorship is not being discussed in quite the same language as among the Fathers of the Constitution in the 18th century or by the social reformers after World War One; nonetheless, we find ourselves at the end of the 20th century dealing with very similar issues, though expressed in more directly industrial terms.

All of the new technology requires government intervention in order to come into existence, whether through the launching of a satellite or the adjudication of an industrial rights matter. We appear to live in an age of transition, but the age could last for a very long time; the new text technologies will continue to arrive for many decades and we are really not discussing a temporary phenomenon but a permanent aspect of the information revolution. What, in American political parlance, is labelled the issue of "deregulation" is really the same thing that in Western Europe is called "regulation"—it is just another stage in the 500-year-old argument about the power of the King over the printing press.

The age of telecommunications requires a special kind of stewardship on the part of bureaucracy, judiciary and executive, over the social condition of information. The intellectual and information highways have to be guaranteed, just as canals, railroads, airways and roads have to be guaranteed and maintained by government, at the end of long processes of consultation with public and industry. There have to be decisions about which side of the road we drive on, how the telecommunications highways are to be built and policed, to protect us against the informational equivalent of the road hog.

The ancient arguments about censorship are therefore not about to disappear in the age of information abundance, when the sheer plurality of means should, in the belief of some, simply overtake all problems of who should be permitted to say what. The arguments are in the process of being intensified. The answers provided by the U.S. Constitution, the Second Reform Act in Britain, the 1881 Press Law of the French Third Republic, are merely turning out to be interim solutions.

There can be no freedom of expression where there is no public right to disseminate moving images with sound freely, and yet there exists no agreement, even in societies committed to free expression, that films and television programs should be free from inspection, certification or complete banning. There can be no real guarantee of equal universal education unless children are taught to handle the new communication systems when they are taught to read. The problem is that the answers given in the past simply cannot be extended into the new conditions. There exists no agreement to that effect and probably none will exist. The whole range of problems have once again to be subjected to an era of debate and legislation.

Creating the Audience

While the state is shouldering greater responsibility for guaranteeing (indeed, creating) the new flows of information, the role of the state as an organizer of audiences appears to be coming to an end. It is an old function of the state, emerging from church and pulpit and later visible in the mandatory education system. It became one of the chief functions of the evolving bureaucracy of industrial societies to oversee, as it were, the manufacturing of audiences.

One may consider mass literacy as a kind of state-manufactured receiving apparatus, the existence of which caused governments to realize there now existed a social obligation to control content. With the arrival of cinema, radio and television, a variety of regulatory mechanisms were devised, each for a different and special reason, some local, some national, some with the intention of controlling morals and mores, others with the intention of guaranteeing physical safety of audiences. All of these systems of intervention became quickly linked to an overall set of bureaucratic concerns for the control of society as audience.

In several countries cinema was regulated merely in order to protect audiences against the dangers of nitrate fires; local authorities were therefore given the sole statutory power to intervene; nonetheless, this system became merely the wedge and a *de facto* state suzerainty rapidly emerged. In Scandinavian countries the anxiety of the authorities was expressed more in the attempt to protect against the infiltration of a foreign dominant culture. This gradually led to a general municipalization of exhibition outlets, something which would not have occurred if cinema had been perceived as an indigenous product (where control over content would be automatically linked to the prevailing apparatuses of social control).

What the state unconsciously accepted as its area of interest, however, was the function of building the pattern of audience composition, as a means of regulating the medium concerned. Thus, Britain's broadcasting system developed alongside conscious and long-debated choices concerning local versus national provision, popular versus highbrow; governmental judgments were made concerning the quantity of instructional material which should be offered and the amount of religious broadcasting. To this day government is involved in precisely the same area of judgment in connection with radio and television in Britain and so are governments in every part of the democratic world. Governmental intervention at this level of audience conceptualization and organization is the only means by which the media of broadcasting can be made to link to democratic institutions.

In the United States where, uniquely, a purely commercial structure was devised for radio and television, the control took the form of an attempt to restrict the nature and size of markets, by laying down a pattern of local signals supervised by the FCC. Through this mechanism a score of other less conscious, less overt, forms of social control came pouring. Pressure was exerted at the level of licensing rather than through the open mechanism of government departments. Very rapidly in country after country the machinery of broadcasting, established in the 1920s and 1930s, partly adapting from measures already taken in the case of cinema, partly deriving from social attitudes and districting systems established in the case of mass education, came to concern itself with the segmenting and arrangement of audiences.

Changing Structures

In the 1980s and 1990s the technological choices made by governments and corporations are likely to lead to a general escape from the structures established in earlier decades. In most societies, audiences are, for the most part, held within an internally competing structure of three or four signals. Even in the United States, until very recently, the vast bulk of the audience has been held by three networks plus the Public Broadcasting Service (PBS) and the odd successful local station. In such systems the pressures towards pluralism are seldom victorious. A concept of the audience-as-a-whole dominates each separate signal: each supplier feels that more is to be gained from the median than the marginal.

However, at a given level of signal-multiplication (perhaps, when there are eight or more competing signals, each accompanied by the necessary promotional activity), the traditional methods for organizing the audiences of a society come to an end. The underlying pressure towards a form of pluralism must take over from the centralizing tendencies of limited competitive systems.

At the same time wholly new technologies for supplying moving images are coming to the fore, which are not easily susceptible to indigenous regulation in any society. The traditional debates concerning local versus national audience, whether to advance mass versus minority taste, rural versus metropolitan, etc., etc., are likely to peter out or to be swamped by some newer cultural debate. We seem to be at the beginning of the end of one important area of work for the apparatus of nation states.

Before returning more directly to our theme of authorship it is important to look more closely at the part played by the state in industrial societies within the flows of information, for there exist a number of unstated assumptions in the process. In absorbing the tasks of education and basic socialization into the work of government, societies took automatic decisions concerning the role of the vernacular, concerning the official status of religious teaching, concerning the career structures of industry and, therefore, the whole outlook of every individual.

In taking on education so totally, government undertook the responsibility for the manufacture, so to speak, of adulthood itself, of defining the elements of social maturity and then of supplying them. Certain implied quantities of information are sufficient to transform childhood into adulthood. Such assumptions regarding information required for participation in society have continued to inhabit the later institutions which carried forward the fight from the mass education systems to the mass broadcasting and entertainment systems.

The "private" elements of national information systems have, to a very great extent, acted as the servicing agents of a state machinery. Publishing and music, for example, are to a great extent dependent upon the education and entertainment structures of a society, as are film production and distribution.

In the current fragmentation of audiences we are witnessing a media process which is also a social (and political) process, a change in the consciousness of audiences emerging from a change in the technical and regulatory control of audiences. The relationship between the "author," who sits at one crucial point in the information flow, and the audience/society is clearly going to change significantly, as the new tendencies work their way through the institutions and supporting industries.

TRANSNATIONALITY OF INFORMATION

Now we come to the fifth of these basic principles of the information process which is today undergoing change. It's a rather difficult one to explain. We are used to information systems, certainly in Western Europe, which are essentially national, unilingual, frequently uniconfessional—i.e., we're used to all the information to which we are subjected as individuals somehow belonging to *our* society, being addressed to us in our own language and very frequently in the light of one set of ethics or one set of religious principles which happen to be the dominant ones of our particular society. That indigenousness goes very deep, is inscribed very deeply in the prevailing notion of citizenship. We think of ourselves as citizens of a given society and thus as the receptacle of certain quantities of information which have accepted those principles of uniconfessionality, unilinguality and uninationality.

However, the age of computerized information and the new information systems is a transnational age. There is no longer the possiblity for sovereignty of knowledge, sovereignty of information being coterminous with the political sovereignty to which the individual citizen is subjected. We live in an age in which transnational corporations and international organizations are the main sources of information and the main distributors of it. And that is the end of another of those very settled principles that have belonged to the era of Gutenberg.

Some time after the turn of the 21st century the coming of automatic translation will deal another heavy blow to this identification of national sovereignty with information. We feel that we have, as citizens, some kind of bureaucracy which determines what may or may not be represented. A very special kind of anomie must evolve in a society whose citizens are bereft of that power. We have all lived through a decade of argument over the public representation of women, blacks, gays and of the concomitant class relationships. The gradual erosion of the machinery of control within a society must inevitably increase rather than diminish certain types of frustration. The age of abundance and choice is also therefore an age of bewilderment and a certain helplessness—a political as well as cultural helplessness.

THE END OF THE MYTH

Those, therefore, are five ways in which the new information environment, the post-Gutenbergian age, differs from the inherited one. All of them are tendencies rather than absolutes; all of them were already evident in previous decades and are accelerated rather than created by the new technologies. All of the changes will play upon the role of the author and help to reorganize the functions performed by the author, as a concept, in society. The author as an eponymous, self-standing being is an illusion necessary to the processes by which information has traditionally been reproduced, stored, distributed.

Before the age of Gutenberg the problem was to preserve knowledge rather than to add to it. Those who had the most important role were essentially the librarians—those who preserved, protected and organized the information. In the modern post-Renaissance age another principle, that of the author, became supreme. The machinery of information was under the titular control of the author. The librarian's techniques served the system which developed around the author as the central guarantor of the text. The computer age is beginning in many ways, some of them subtle, some of them quite dramatic, to unwind that concept of authorship.

I think it is becoming apparent that information is a kind of common property and belongs to entire communities, at least in its latent stage. Books are compiled from other books. Writers are locked inside their language and their literary heritage, their tradition. They purify the language of the tribe, as Eliot said. That's called authorship. In the age of the computer, the real, the undiscovered, the concealed structures will become clearer. Texts come into existence, as the result of collective actions by numberless individuals and institutions spread around the world.

The myths around authorship are in a sense being exploded both in technology and in the field of law. Copyright belongs essentially to an age when information was dominated by the concept of authorship, and with the erosion of the semi-sacral character of authorship comes a better recognition of the collective social nature of information and of culture. The demise of authors is of course not being predicted, more the image of authors, the separation of authors from the apparatus by which they are known.

Of course, we have been looking at only one tiny part of the impact of the new information technologies. Perhaps what we have been mainly doing is working through a method by which to evaluate and measure the changes taking place. If one looks too closely at events, however, their implications remain obscure, and it is possible to look at the welter of technical change of the 1980s as if its effects were merely of scale rather than kind. Scale is the most trivial of them, however.

What they represent in aggregate is the promise of change in the nature of selfhood, in the instrument by which we look upon the world and know it and by which it absorbs us. Between us and it comes the screen of representations, of statements about the world and our place in it, both visual and verbal statements, which fashion in turn our consciousness and which are in their turn altered by the manner in which we understand them.

We label the processes of interaction "education" or, more modernly, "socialization"—a set of habits or reflexes set within the psyche itself. At the level of their social expansion we call these culture. We should not pretend that purely technological changes can transform culture; they can only work alongside the processes of culture and filter them. But at our present juncture something indeed appears to be happening on the grander scale of which the technological component is evidence rather than cause, a general reconstitution of the information procedures of the world. That must shift the location of many of the fixed points in the mental environment, not least upon the concept of authorship and the place of authorship within the structuring of knowledge.

4

Publishing and the New Technology

by Dan Lacy

A good way to begin a consideration of the impact of the new electronic technology on publishing, especially book publishing, is to ask what books are good for anyway. Part of the answer has to be that different books are good for different things. Some are to be read as a whole, whether for pleasure, for enlightenment or for understanding; examples are novels, biographies, histories, treatises in philosophy or politics or science. Some, like textbooks, are to be studied. Others, like dictionaries, cookbooks, encyclopedias and handbooks, are for reference—collections of data looked up and used one item at a time.

CHARACTERISTICS OF BOOKS

All of these books have certain common characteristics, whether strengths or weaknesses:

1. They are *extensive* bodies of information, whether they are integrated wholes (*Huckleberry Finn*) or aggregations of discrete data (*Webster's New Collegiate Dictionary*), perhaps typically 3 to 10 million bits (roughly 190 to 625 pages). Less than half a million bits can hardly be called a book at all.

2. They are generally viable only if a market of *several thousand purchasers* is available for the total aggregate of information in an identical form.

3. They are *fixed*, and additions or corrections of the data contained can be achieved only at the cost of a whole new edition.

4. They are *slow* to produce, and the information in a book is typically several months old at the very moment of publication.

5. Though alphabetical or chronological arrangement can make it easy to locate an individual fact in a book if the approach is a standard one (e.g., knowing the spelling of a word, you seek its pronunciation, etymology or definition), and though indexes enhance searchability, books *do not usually offer alternative or unforeseen* approaches to individual items in their content. Crossword puzzle or double-crostic fans, for example, can not call up from a dictionary a list of seven-letter words whose fourth letter is "l" and whose seventh is "g."

Books have several clearly positive characteristics:

1. Books are *inexpensive*. A college dictionary is a data base of perhaps 15 million or more bits that sells for $11.95, with no further charges for access. This is an incomparably lower cost than that of accessing an electronic data base each time one wanted to look up a word.

2. Books are *convenient*. They are easily portable and require no apparatus or connection to be read.

3. Books are, or can be, *esthetically pleasing*, or at any rate unobtrusive, so that one can read at length from a book more comfortably than one can read at length from a screen or a computer printout.

CHARACTERISTICS OF ELECTRONIC DATA BASES

The characteristics of electronic data bases are for the most part reciprocal to those of books. That is, the limitations of one are the strengths of the other. Though an electronic data base can contain an unlimited amount of information, it comes into tangible and visible being only as an expression of the particular datum or segment called for by the user. Unlike books, data bases deal with parts rather than wholes.

The particular material called forth from the data base responds to the particular inquiry of an individual user— selected, perhaps manipulated, and formatted to his specifications. It serves an audience of one where the book requires thousands.

Moreover, the electronic data base can be instantly and continuously updated so that it never need be lacking in currency. And the particular extract or assemblage of extracts the user requires can be presented to him immediately, without the long delays of publication.

On the other hand, electronic data bases are expensive. Over a period of time one can look up a thousand words in a college dictionary for slightly more than a penny apiece; to consult an electronic data base of words a thousand times would be likely to cost thousands of dollars in equipment rental, connect time and line charges.

Electronic data bases are physically inconvenient, in that they can be consulted only through the intermediary of relatively cumbersome, usually not portable, terminals electronically connected to the data base. And they are irksome to read for any extended period.

THE STRENGTH OF THE BOOK

This sketchy analysis suggests that there are only certain functions that books serve well, leaving an enormous area of service for the new electronic media, which do superbly many things books cannot do at all or do very poorly. But it also suggests that books still perform better than any other medium the services within their special competence.

In particular, the work that is intended to be read as a

whole and that can command an audience of several thousand will continue to be more effectively disseminated in traditional book form—inexpensive, compact, portable, requiring no equipment to use, and pleasing to handle and read. And this is the great majority of all books. They are not likely to be replaced or indeed seriously affected by any of the new computer-based technologies. Such competition as they encounter from the electronic world is indirect, in the competition for recreational time and attention. Book reading has faced this competition in one form or another throughout the century: bicycling, motoring, sports, the movies, radio and television have successively drawn on the attention and time that might otherwise have been devoted to the reading of books. Books have survived, and experience suggests that on balance television may indeed have stimulated rather than inhibited their use.

Opportunities for entertainment and recreation in the home will be enhanced by multichannel cable and by video cassettes and video discs, which will offer a far wider diversity of choice than traditional network fare. Electronic games will provide further options. This greater choice may increase the number of potential readers drawn from books to the video screen, but the change is not likely to be dramatic; the primary competition will be rather between the new visual media and traditional television.

ON-DEMAND PRINTING

The new technology does offer a new range of opportunities for the book-length work that cannot attract a sufficient readership to justify its publication in traditional format. So-called "on-demand" printing allows the material to be stored in the form of an extremely compact and inexpensive "master" from which individual copies are produced as desired. There is nothing radically new about this: an earlier technology, microphotography, has already afforded this opportunity. Indeed, almost as many books are published annually in an "on-demand" mode in the United States as are published traditionally. Half a million doctoral dissertations have been copyrighted, cataloged and "published" by University Microfilms alone. Negative microfilms of the typed dissertations are filed; detailed catalogs are issued; and positive films are enlarged and bound paper copies supplied on demand with royalties to the authors.

More recent computer-based technology simply offers an opportunity to facilitate this process by affording an even cheaper and more compact storage medium in the laser disc and by providing better bibliographical control through online searches of bibliographic data bases and the opportunity of immediate online delivery through a terminal printer. Institutional arrangements comparable to those of University Microfilms have not yet been created to do all this, but probably will be. The advent of University Microfilms service hastened the disappearance of the already dying practice of requiring the printing of dissertations, and to that extent may be said to have replaced some traditional publishing of complete texts. The newer technologies may extend this process by pushing further the margin below which on-demand publishing will be the preferred method. But the principal consequence of the use of both microfilm and the newer technologies is not to replace print, but to allow the publication of works that otherwise could not have been published at all.

COST REDUCTIONS FOR JOURNAL PUBLISHERS

The impact of the newer technologies is likely to be more strongly felt in the case of journals than in that of books. Promptness is more important, and the brevity of individual articles makes format less so. But the principal advantage of the new technology with respect to journal publication, or more precisely with respect to the publication of journal articles, is its capacity to lower transaction costs.

The typical contribution to scientific knowledge, and to a lesser extent to other academic areas, is the 2500 to 7500 word document. (This is in contrast to the book-length work characteristic of history, biography and fiction.) High transaction costs have hitherto made impractical the separate publication of such brief documents. Publishers could not afford the marketing expense of handling each of hundreds or thousands of articles as a separate venture, nor could the bibliographic resources of scholars and the cataloging capacity of libraries deal with them individually. The solution was to package them in journals. A nearly automatically renewed subscription could solve the marketing problem of publishers and the acquisitions problems of libraries and individual scholars, as one transaction could cover an indefinitely large number of articles with advance commitments. And one catalog entry plus a serial record could establish a library's bibliographic control over the physical artifacts, so that the library could rely on the journal's internal indexes and table of contents plus external tools (e.g., other indexes and bibliographies) to lead to individual articles.

The computer, with its radical lowering of clerical costs, has dramatically reduced the transaction costs that have imposed the journal format. It would be quite practical to continue the editorial and disciplinary function of scientific and scholarly journals by having articles submitted for publication as they are now. They could be edited and referred for peer review as they are now. Accepted articles could be read by an optical scanner and stored in machine-readable format, probably in a laser disc. The author, title, abstract and keyword subject headings could be entered in a bibliographic data base, which could be searched online by an inquirer, or could be continually screened for relevant new entries conforming to a user's pre-entered profile. The text of any desired article could be reviewed on a terminal screen or printed out on a terminal printer. Browsing needs could be met if necessary by the publication in traditional form of tables of contents with brief abstracts, though automatic screening on the basis of user profiles would serve most of this need.

Though clearly there will continue to be a need for general magazines and trade journals and for more broadly circulated scientific and scholarly journals, the system described above could radically alter the mode of disseminating articles now published in specialized journals of limited circulation. Indeed, since automatic screening would pick up articles in any definite sector of interest, a single publishing mechanism could consolidate the administrative (though not the selective and peer review) functions of many specialized journals.

THE LASER DISC

Digitized recording in laser disc form may also provide a new medium for the publication of book-length works with features that cannot be fully embodied in print. These include works describing motion and sounds. Works on music appreciation, for example, in laser disc form could roll the text across the screen to the accompaniment of the music discussed. Houghton Mifflin is said to be experimenting with the incorporation of a field guide to birds in disc and cassette format, which could include the text, recordings of bird songs, and depictions of the bird in flight. Travel and architecture books afford similar possibilities. This is not really novel; the same possibilities have long existed in film and more recently in video cassettes. But the expense and inconvenience of this means of publication is likely to continue to confine it to very specialized uses.

The same technology, however, is likely to have a broader use in education, particularly in training courses to impart specific skills. Even here video discs and cassettes, like the already familiar training films, are more likely to complement than to replace printed texts. Successful training requires an opportunity for the learner to see the actual performance of the operation to be learned, indeed to see it repeatedly. It also requires an opportunity for the learner to practice for a greater or lesser number of times depending on his learning pace, and to have his performance checked, his errors pointed out and explained, and his successes acknowledged. All this is impossible with a textbook alone, and is a tedious and expensive use of a teacher's time.

A training film or video cassette can give the opportunity for repeated observation. But a more effective training device will be a terminal connected with a computer-assisted laser disc with random access, stop-frame and branching capacities. This will enable each student to work independently and at his own pace, to recall the text—in words, sound and motion pictures—as often as he wishes, to answer questions or solve problems with immediate and nonjudgmental feedback and to do so as often as necessary, and finally to be led along the learning path best suited to his ability, learning style and mastery of earlier material.

It is expensive and intellectually demanding to produce training materials conforming to this ideal, and their effective use requires large numbers of relatively expensive terminals. Moreover, as learning tools, they are more effective in teaching specific skills to motivated students than in educating in a broader sense. Hence they are likely to find their largest use, at least in the near future, in the training programs of large corporations, perhaps government agencies and such institutions as hospitals. Moreover, they are more likely to replace or supplement unstructured informal teaching of an apprenticeship type than to replace formal textbooks. Individualized disc or cassette instruction in the public schools is likely to be the subject of active and extensive discussion and comment, but very limited actual use in the near future.

"LOOK-UP" FUNCTIONS

The real contest between books and computer-based information technology, if indeed there is one, is in the field of those books that are designed to be consulted rather than read, from which the reader seeks a specific item or a concise element of information rather than an extended text. Dictionaries, encyclopedias, handbooks, statistical compilations, transportation schedules and directories are examples of this type of book. The information in such a book is, of course, a data base. It can reside on a magnetic tape cassette or disc or in a computer's memory bank as well as in print. Indeed, such data bases now usually exist on tape or disc at one stage in the process of embodying them in print.

Given the appropriate terminals, networks and applications software, the user can address his query "online" to the computer data base instead of looking it up in the book. He could, for example, type the word MESOMORPH on his terminal keyboard and have the syllabification, pronunciation, etymology and definition appear on the screen. This would seem an expensive and impractical procedure, as compared with looking the word up in a dictionary.

A similar but more practical application would be an electronic directory where the data change frequently (sometimes daily) and constant updates are desirable. The French national telephone service is in fact considering abandoning printed telephone directories and substituting inexpensive terminals at each telephone instrument; the inquirer could keyboard the name of the person he seeks to reach and have the number appear on the terminal screen. Directories of business organizations, associations, financial statistics, etc. are other examples of this type.

More complex operations of "looking up" by online access to a data base are more practical and in fact are already in very widespread use. Most of those most widely used, however, replace the task of looking up a fact in a paper file rather than in a book: for example, finding the current balance in a bank account, validating a credit card, verifying an airline reservation, checking the status of a customer's account with a utility, learning the most recent trading price of a stock. In all these cases, the need for up-to-the-minute data makes print an obviously impossible medium. Indeed for most of them, even paper files would be quite impractical, and the present level of operations is made possible only by the use of online data bases.

Bibliographic Data Bases

Other look-up uses, however, do involve data bases that are or have been maintained in print as well. The earliest and most extensive employment of this medium with respect to printed data bases was in the field of bibliography. Such enormous reference works as the INDEX MEDICUS, which attempted to list and index almost all significant articles in the biomedical literature, American and foreign, fell increasingly behind with manual methods of preparation. To preserve its value as a current guide to literature, it became necessary to use the computer for sorting entries, preparing indexes and typesetting for current issues and periodic cumulations. Once the entries were in machine-readable form, batch processing could be undertaken to give any inquirer a printout listing articles conforming to his criteria. And finally, through MEDLINE, the data base was opened to online access.

Literally hundreds of other bibliographic data bases have now been made available online, both in the United States and abroad, in general through the use of such networks and applications software as System Development Corp.'s Orbit or Lockheed Information Service's Dialog. Online catalogs, replacing the traditional card catalog, are following in larger research institutions.

Full-Text Access

Online access has been extended from bibliographies to texts themselves. Perhaps the principal application to date has been in the legal field. Here the largest service is LEXIS, owned by Mead Data Central, though the West Publishing Company's WESTLINE and two services of Federal agencies, JURIS and LITES, offer somewhat similar services. These services enable an inquirer to search through the texts of statutes and appellate court decisions for any that contain key words, singly or in various combinations, identifying the subject of concern; to view the paragraphs containing the identifying words so that he can verify their relevance; and finally to have the full text displayed page-by-page on the screen or printed out by a printer.

Such a service can indeed replace the printed volumes of statutes and appellate court reports. In practice, however, they rarely do. The advantage of such systems is not in the storage and presentation of the text, at which print remains superior, but in their indexing power. Having identified the relevant cases, the lawyer typically will turn to printed reports, if they are available, to study, analyze and annotate the opinion. If the books are not available, he will get a printout from the system rather than work from the screen.

Newspapers and Magazines

Similar full-text systems have also been used for general news reports. Such services as the New York Times Information Bank, NEXIS, Dow Jones News/Retrieval Service, GLOBE DATA and DATA COURIER, INC., make available the full texts or abstracts of the content of a number of newspapers, magazines and news services through indexing, display and printout services comparable to those of LEXIS. Such services are more likely than LEXIS, however, to replace reference to the original printed version. Newspapers are bulky, printed on paper quick to disintegrate, and in general difficult to preserve; magazines are only somewhat less so. Though most large law firms will have at hand or in a nearby law library sets of the statutes and case reports more frequently used, few subscribers to NEXIS would have available back files of all the magazines and newspapers covered. Even when back files of newspapers are available in a library convenient to the system's user, they are likely to be on microfilm. In such a case it will usually be more convenient to obtain a printout from the system than from the library.

Though they may replace the use of back files, however, systems like the Information Bank and NEXIS do not in any way replace the current issues of newpapers or magazines. Agreements between the publisher and the system often prohibit the release of material from any issue of a newspaper or magazine through the system until it has become non-current. But even in the absence of such an agreement, technical problems of entering the material would make it impossible for the online system to deliver news concurrently with the newspaper from which it is drawn and difficult even to stay current with magazines.

The peculiar virtue of all systems like LEXIS, the Information Bank and NEXIS is not their capacity to store and deliver material in the first instance. In this they are likely to be inferior to print. Their virtue is rather in their powerful indexing capability and in their ability to scan a wide variety of sources and bring together from all of them whatever is relevant to any particular inquiry. This is not a capacity to do better what print has done and hence to replace it; it is rather a new capacity adding to the resources available to inquirers.

Some have foreseen the replacement of print in another way, by the availability in the home of videotext services. Among these would be a continuous news service, displaying text scrolled or rolled across a screen or continuously printed out, which might replace the newspaper. This is actually not a new phenomenon. Teletype machines, continuously clattering out the news, have long been available for any who need and can afford them. Televised news in pictorial form now reaches almost every home in America and has indeed already replaced the newspaper as the principal source of news for most Americans. However, except that it has undoubtedly added to the many problems of evening newspapers, it has not driven newspapers from the field, as the papers seem to serve rather different needs: for fuller and more detailed news, for specialized news (chess columns, baseball box scores, stock market quotations, etc.), for advertising that can be read and compared and for leisurely browsing.

THE LIMITED IMPACT OF ELECTRONIC PUBLISHING

There is nothing in the evidence of numbers to suggest that the flow of print is contracting under the impact of the new technology. In 1950, when the impact of television first began to be felt, 11,022 books were published in the United States. In 1970, when the impact of the computer began to reach major proportions, the number of books had risen to 36,071. In 1979, after almost 30 years of television and 10 years of major computer use, 45,182 books were published in the United States. Book publishing revenues in the United States in 1950 were less than $500 million; in 1970 they were more than $2.9 billion; in 1980, more than $7.0 billion.

Where the two modes of dissemination come into competition is along the fringes of print's utility — that is, at the point where barely enough copies are needed to make print practicable. Just as the printing of doctoral dissertations long ago yielded to microfilm from typescript, the highly specialized journal may migrate to the video disc and the computer. But since we are dealing with products of the most limited edition size, the impact on the core of commercial publishing will be very small indeed. The fortunes of books may suffer in the future, but not because of computers or videotext.

Some writers who might agree with this conservative estimate would nevertheless contend that the propects for electronic publishing in the near future are limited primarily by the facts that very few homes have terminals and that even where suitable terminals exist in businesses and institutions, their use is unfamiliar. These analysts anticipate that when terminals have become generally available and widely familiar, electronic publishing will increase so dramatically as to perform a wholly new range of functions.

I think not. Certainly as society is more widely supplied with appropriate terminals, there will be greatly increased use of electronic publishing for those functions for which its efficiency has already been demonstrated. More lawyers will use LEXIS, more corporate libraries will call on the New York Times Information Bank, more researchers will call upon computerized bibliographies. In business and professional offices more and more data, especially information on current transactions, will flow electronically.

But I remain skeptical that this wider and more frequent use of already demonstrated potential will be accompanied by important new or different uses. I am particularly skeptical about the use, even in the long term, of home terminals to provide information flows comparable to those now provided by books, magazines and newspapers. The higher costs and the inconvenience of reading from a terminal or printout will continue to limit electronic publishing to those areas in which immediacy of delivery or powerful indexing capacity are essential. These demands are rare except in business and professional use, and I would anticipate that the home terminal will continue to be used primarily for entertainment and possibly for transactional purposes such as bill-paying, banking and shopping, rather than as a replacement for books, magazines or newspapers.

MAJOR IMPLICATIONS FOR PUBLISHERS

Though we may feel some confidence that the newer technologies are not likely to displace print from its true central function in the publication of editions of books, magazines or newpapers of commercially viable size, they nevertheless are of great importance to publishers. The new technology has, or is likely to have, very important implications for the way texts are prepared and manufactured as books, journals or magazines, and for the way they are preserved after their initial use is ended.

Text Preparation

The computer, by offering an almost unbelievable ability to manipulate and array data, adds enormous power to the creator of many kinds of works, whether he is the editor of a Biblical concordance, an econometric historian, a statistical analyst of public opinion, or the editor of a dictionary. Coupled with word-processing equipment, the computer may change many of the routine processes of publishing. Manuscripts can be input into tape, or more likely disc, format either by keyboarding in the publisher's office or by optical character recognition scanning equipment. A few authors skilled in the new technology already submit manuscripts on machine-readable tape; more will undoubtedly do so in the future. Editing of such "manuscripts" will be done on a terminal; and the revised tape, without further keyboarding, can produce camera-ready copy in any desired typeface and layout. The publisher will in effect often take over the typesetting functions now performed in the composing room of printing houses.

The procedures have already become almost standard practice for newspapers and are widely employed for news magazines and other staff-written journals. Application to the work of outside authors will follow, bringing reductions in both editing and plant costs. In many smaller ways as well, new computer technology is improving the efficiency of the whole production process. And through computerized inventory controls and royalty and other accounting systems it is substantially reducing general operating costs.

Marketing

Marketing has also been made much more efficient by the use of the computer. The assignment of sales territories, the control of lists for the mailing of complimentary and review copies, the maintenance of specialized mailing lists and targeting of sales calls—all have been made much easier. The ability to handle single-copy sales with lower transactions costs will also encourage more direct marketing. For periodicals publishers, the computer has also made it practical to split up the single runs of magazines with large circulations and to provide separate runs for particular regions or even metropolitan areas. Advertising space can be sold separately for each such run, enabling publishers to sell advertising competitively with spot sales of TV time. All in all, the computer and other new technologies have done much and will do more to restrain the costs and increase the efficiency of print publishing.

Library Use

The new technology will have special implications for libraries that will, in turn, affect publishers. Technology may in time afford answers to the twin problems of preservation of printed materials—space and longevity. Earlier microfilm technology is universally used to preserve newspapers, which are exceptionally bulky and expensive to store and which are on quickly deteriorating newsprint. Video discs will afford a more compact and easily retrieved medium for the storage of noncurrent or infrequently used materials, and libraries may come to use them extensively for that purpose. Discs will have two additional advantages over microfilm for this purpose. One is that most printed materials now, and undoubtedly nearly all in the future, will have been put into digital form as a part of the printing process and can be recorded on a disc as a master copy at relatively nominal expense at that time. Other discs can be reproduced cheaply for libraries that want to use them for storage, initially no doubt of noncurrent newspaper, magazine and journal files. The other advantage is that discs can readily be searched in any one of a number of modes and can conveniently produce hard-copy printouts from printers attached to terminals.

Libraries are being and will be affected by the new technologies in other ways that have important meaning for publishers. The computer can greatly enlarge the efficiency of libraries, enabling them to create and maintain catalogs more effectively, to extend their bibliographic reach and to bring new services to their users. But these very achievements, requiring as they do heavy new investments, generally substantially increase library operating costs. At a time of increasingly severe budgetary constraints, this additional cost indirectly reduces funds available for the acquisition of printed materials.

The cost of providing online services to library users raises special problems. Many librarians feel strongly that the traditions of free library service require that access to data bases through a library's terminals be offered without charge in order to provide equal access to information without discrimination on the basis of ability to pay. But since most users of online data bases are likely to be relatively well-off businessmen, professionals and researchers, pursuing such a policy might mean that funds otherwise available for printed materials to serve the library's needier constituency would instead be diverted to the service of those better able to pay.

As in the analogous case of providing photocopies, libraries may compromise by passing on direct or incremental costs to the user and absorbing indirect costs. But in any event, the use of the newer technologies, those essential to the future of libraries, is likely to reduce somewhat the library's relative importance as a market for print publications. This will have a special impact on university presses, scholarly journals and in general publishers of serious nonfiction.

Impact On Advertising Revenue

There is, however, one other major impact that the new technology may have on the print media—not in replacing the media themselves but in diverting the advertising revenue on which at least newspapers and many magazines depend for survival. Television itself has already demonstrated this potential effect. Watching television did not rob *Life* or *Look* or *The Saturday Evening Post* or *Colliers* or the *American Magazine* of audience, or at least not of so much of their audience as to make them no longer viable. But television did for the first time provide a mass nationwide means of advertising products visually, a function hitherto possible only through nationally circulated mass magazines. A large enough proportion of mass national advertising shifted from magazines to television — following a smaller earlier migration to radio—to have a serious impact on the mass popular magazine. Many, already troubled by other difficulties, failed.

The magazine industry has recovered from this heavy blow, largely by strengthening editorial quality, increasing the proportion of income from subscribers and seeking specialized approaches that would single out audiences by sex, age, income level, style and interests in a way impossible to television. Though television became the dominant means of advertising such universally consumed products as automobiles, beer, shampoos, deodorants, home appliances, coffee and the like, magazines retained a powerful role in advertising aimed at select audiences, such as those of *The New Yorker* or *Business Week*, or specialized ones, like the readers of magazines on tennis, yachting, cooking, personal computers or other hobbies.

Television has also proved to be more effective as a national than as a local medium because the great expense of preparing commercials needs to be amortized against a broad national use. In part for the same reason, it is also more effective as an advertiser of national brands than of individual stores or specific sales. Though local television stations have won an increasing amount of advertising from banks, savings and loan associations, automobile dealers, furniture stores, drug and fast food chains and local firms wanting to advertise the establishment rather than a specific item, newspapers have remained by far the dominant medium for local advertising. This has been particularly true for department and clothing stores wanting to advertise special sales or particular items for classified ads.

The advertising revenues of both specialized magazines and newspapers are now challenged by new technological developments. Satellite distribution to multi-channel cable systems for the first time may come to afford advertisers an opportunity to use the television set, like the magazine, as an instrument to reach specialized audiences. Sports networks, women's interest networks, cultural networks, ethnic and foreign language programming, are particularly likely to appeal to such advertisers. Though it can never offer the hundreds, indeed thousands, of specialized audiences reached by different magazines, "narrowcasting" with the audiovisual potential of television and a higher degree of selectivity may become a significant advertising medium, with a marginal but perceptible effect on magazines.

Potentially more important is the effect of the new technology on newspaper advertising. Videotext technology using two-way cable or the telephone system may enable the viewer to seek out advertising in which he is specifically interested, as he can with a newspaper but cannot with conventional TV. Classified advertisements would be especially vulnerable. And if the system includes a capacity to respond and actually place an order, the competitive strength of television would be great. Very few cable systems have such a capacity and it is expensive to install. Immediate change in the competitive situation is not imminent. A likely outcome is that newspapers may themselves use and derive advertising revenue from cable for those functions in which it is especially effective.

CONCLUSION

In summary, publishers of printed works will find powerful uses of the new technology in the production, marketing and delivery of their products; librarians, scientists and scholars will find additional means of disseminating works too specialized for print and for preserving and maintaining access to those no longer in active use; educators may find a useful auxiliary tool. But is is very unlikely indeed that the new technology will replace print in any of those core functions which it efficiently performs.

To put it another way, the new computer, telecommunication and video disc technologies will substitute for print in certain areas that lie along the margins of print's competences. But their principal effects will be, on the one hand, to afford kinds of information dissemination not possible by the use of print and hence not previously available, and on the other, to make the production, marketing and delivery of printed works much more economical and efficient and to provide some marginal added income to publishers from the secondary distribution of information from their printed products. Though there may be some diversion of advertising income, on balance, print publishers have much more to gain than to fear from the new technology.

5

Libraries: A New Role?

by Robert D. Stueart

The invention of movable type in 1456 challenged libraries to become purveyors of knowledge through the mass medium of the written word in a print-on-paper format. That development came just in time, because mankind's knowledge base had become too voluminous to be recorded and passed on through meticulously hand-copied manuscripts or through the oral tradition. Libraries thus took on a new role: the dissemination of information produced in book form.

Today libraries must be prepared to take on another new role, making use of electronic technologies that produce and disseminate information in many and varied formats. Electronic publishing, online information retrieval, microforms, the optical video disc, videotext services, and advanced telecommunications technologies such as satellite transmission are aspects of an electronic revolution that is changing the ways in which information is generated, stored and transferred. This revolution has already brought about more change in libraries than any force since the invention of printing. It will continue to change the nature and mission of libraries, unless they wish to be regarded as warehouses or as distribution centers for those who cannot afford to buy books.

THE CHANGING CONCEPT OF THE LIBRARY

Eighteenth century attitudes toward libraries and librarians are succinctly stated in *The Old Librarian's Almanac,* allegedly written in 1773, which describes the librarian's profession as the "goodliest of all occupations"—the pursuit of wisdom. Librarians, in that treatise, were admonished to make sure the users of their collections were persons of "good reputation, scholarly habit, sober and courteous demeanor, no mere triflers, no persons who would dally with books" and certainly no persons who would seek in them shallow amusement.

For many observers this image seems to have survived the centuries, even though most libraries in developed nations have changed as they have been caught up in an age where both access to information and the knowledge of how to use it have become important factors in the society's development. At a slower rate than many would have liked, libraries in many parts of the world have begun to assume a newly revised role in a sophisticated information transfer process.

This, however, is not universally true. As one studies comparative librarianship, it becomes evident that libraries begin to play an important role only at a certain stage in a country's development. This point can be evidenced by: the creation of both a national library and a national bibliography; the enactment of library laws by government; program development for the education of library workers; and creation of an indigenous library journal. Libraries in some parts of the world have not yet begun to play that important educational/informational role and are not yet caught up in the technological developments. It is unlikely that some of them will develop to that level within the near future. Universal access to a speedier information system is still remote.

However, in some parts of the world, including the United States, the library profession has moved from a print-on-paper orientation to a more modified one dealing with media in various formats. Still, librarians and users of libraries have been slow to accept the concept of a library as the *service function* that is performed inside those hallowed walls, rather than the *building* itself and its function as a preservation monument. This general acceptance has been an evolutionary process, causing stress, and forced as much by economic, physical and other outside pressures as by a service commitment on the part of librarians. These factors along with recent technological developments, are changing the perception of the library's role.

The Impetus for Change

In 1935, Arthur Fremont Rider, a leading researcher, estimated that the academic library's materials double in number every 15 years. This calculation led to a projection that by the year 2040 Yale University's collection would number 200 million volumes, occupying 6000 miles of shelves. Clearly, the time is fast approaching when space needs for many large libraries are prohibitive, forcing some to seek drastic solutions, including zero-growth of library collections. Added to that staggering statistic is the cold economic fact that the cost of library print-on-paper materials has been increasing at astronomical rates, further stretching the already declining materials budgets of many libraries. During the last several years that portion of the library's budget for subscriptions, which are often priced higher for libraries than for individuals, has become larger than for monographs. This profile suggests that libraries will become much more selective in their purchases of printed materials, whether for information, recreation or education.

To these cost factors must be added the outside pressures of other information agencies, often for-profit, threatening to usurp what has been traditionally thought of as the library's purview. Partly due to the threat of circumvention by information vendors and by information entrepreneurs, some libraries have made a quick advance. For example, some public libraries and community college libraries have become community information centers, providing information and referral services. By so doing, they have revamped the service role of libraries, which have not always been the transfer point between such nontraditional information services and the library user who needs them. Special libraries, particularly in for-profit organizations, have geared their services to information-seeking professionals in the corporation, and librarians have assumed a broader role as information managers. This type of information consultantship will become more prevalent and essential, and will require a variety of information access formats to provide the latest, most accurate and most objective information at all levels of sophistication for a variety of users in a variety of library settings.

NEW INFORMATION FORMATS

Although libraries are still basically print-oriented organizations in an electronic society, their shift toward access to information in various formats came long before the current obsession with electronic data. More than 50 years ago the microcard was "discovered" as having potential for libraries eventually to be "housed in shoeboxes." Later developments of other media propelled the concept of the library's role from a restricted one of supplying "the right book to the right person at the right time" toward that of supplying "the right information to the right person at the right time in the right format and for the right use." It is evident that multiple media (hardcover and paperback books, film, microform, video tape, magnetic tape, radio or television programs, computerized learning programs, etc.) have been the library's stock for some time.

These developments did not diminish the value of the printed word in libraries, but simply reinforced the notion that information comes in many packages, prompting libraries and librarians to be more versatile in order to provide the information in an appropriate format for the user's need. The time has long since passed when libraries were simply collections of books, only one of the media that permit the transmission of ideas from one person to another, from author or editor to reader.

Substitution of electronically stored or microform output text for books and other resources is now a viable alternative for some specialized materials. Development of the video disc, on which books, journals, architectural drawings and other library materials are already being stored, is another alternative that has an attraction for conversion of retrospective library materials.

Electronic Publishing

There has been much talk in recent years about the coming of the "paperless society," and the replacement of print publications by the "electronic journal," "electronic book," etc. Libraries are enthusiastic about developments in technology that will bring electronic publishing of some full-text materials, as well as secondary sources, into reality. At present, however, relatively little full-text material, as opposed to citations and abstracts, is available. The National Enquiry into Scholarly Communication[1] concludes that scholarly journals are not likely to be dislodged from their essential role in the communication of information. Particularly in the sciences, where there is a higher demand for articles related to well-defined research needs, including commercial ones, electronic and microfilm publishing are likely to increase. But as a means of keeping up with the field, these alternatives cannot yet supplant the print journal. As one humanist stated in the Enquiry's interview study, "technology should not intrude on the way that the scholar goes about the conduct of research."

---

1. *Scholarly Communications: The Report of the National Enquiry* (Baltimore, MD: Johns Hopkins Press, 1979).

Such a naive attitude must change as research techniques are altered by advances in technology. The quality of scholarship will continue to depend partly on the rapid availability of a comprehensive full-text collection in whatever form. To some extent, electronic publications are more useful to scientists, whose work is predominantly with recent developments, than to humanists or social scientists, whose work is more hierarchical, spanning a longer period of time. The differences in approaches of these scholars and researchers will require continued attention from libraries, particularly those in academic institutions.

Electronic publishing can allow materials to be produced piecemeal, on demand; for example, one might obtain a particular journal article, rather than the complete journal. This would enable libraries to store fewer low-demand materials. Libraries might begin to use a portion of their acquisitions budgets to purchase hardcopy printouts, either from publishers or from other libraries. These would be one-time-use materials; they could be given to the user at less cost to the library than it would take to process and store an actual volume. Under such circumstances libraries would fill a quasi-publishing role, producing on-demand, electronically transmitted materials whose copyrights are owned by others.

Resistance to materials available only in electronic form is likely to come from potential users who maintain that the machine limits access, becoming a barrier between the material and the reader; it is inconvenient to use; its use is limited to particular places; it causes eye strain; and it has the possibility of "crashing" at an inconvenient time. These reasons are the same ones that microform use has experienced since its inception.

Along with a general trend toward specialization there has been a spate of special interest journals in law, medicine, business, engineering, etc., and a demise of some popular mass interest ones. More researchers now turn first to these specialized journals both for publication of their own findings and as information sources, thereby enabling a speedier turnaround time from information generator to consumer. Fry and White[2] state that in the scientific and academic communities authors write in part for the dissemination of their ideas and results. They also write in part for the recognition toward tenure and advancement which authorship brings them. It therefore appears that the acceptance of more informal, faster and potentially less expensive publication alternatives, such as electronic publishing, hinges on the acceptance of such alternatives as being full-fledged scholarly and research publications.

Microform

There are now extensive resources available in microform: ERIC, HRAF Area Files, government documents, National Technical Information Service (NTIS) publications and *The New York Times,* to mention only a few. In addition, microform publishing of such retrospective series as *English Books Printed Before 1640* and the *American Bibliography* has been instituted for ready access and for preservation purposes. The potential of microfilm for preservation, space saving, reproduction and cost saving has enabled the microform publishing industry to grow from $5 million in 1960 to about $500 million in 1980.

THE LIBRARY AND THE BOOK

Toffler, in *The Third Wave,* admonishes that "the most basic raw material of all—and one that can never be exhausted—is information including imagination. With information becoming more important than ever before, the new civilization

---

2. Bernard M. Fry and Herbert S. White, *Publishers and Libraries: The Study of Scholarly and Research Journals* (Lexington, MA: Lexington Books, 1976).

will restructure education, redefine scientific research and, above all, reorganize the media of communication."[3] Libraries have begun to adjust to the reorganized communications media and are in the process of redefining their own role, which will become enhanced rather than eliminated.

Various other writers have talked about the "Third Scenario," the "Fourth Revolution" and "Era III," all predicting the future. Although it is not the intent of this author to attempt such prophecies or to invent the future for libraries, it is evident that the velocity of change has forced a reexamination of the library's role in the network of knowledge. Knowledge that is derived from the human process of analyzing and understanding information has traditionally been disseminated through a one-way communications channel, the book—or at least print-on-paper. The library has been the preserver, organizer and disseminator of knowledge in an orderly and cumulative form. It has been the place where people who write books and those who read them come to get their information, their education, their enjoyment.

For transmitting knowledge it is doubtful that the printed word can be supplanted easily because it has so many advantages—privately retrievable, portable, absorbable at the individual's own rate and easily handled. Along with other media, it should survive to satisfy a variety of personal learning styles. The book, repository of the experience and learning mankind has accumulated in the past, will continue to be stored in libraries, which have also stood the test of time. One should ask, then: If such an institution has survived for so long with such a collection and with such a mission, should it contemplate changing its primary purpose—of access to knowledge, or preservation of thought and of varied points of view, of cultivation of the mind—to one oriented simply to rapid access to information?

---

3. Alvin Toffler, *The Third Wave* (New York: William Morrow & Co., 1980).

But libraries are also challenged with providing universal access to the widest range of current and objective information. Because of technological developments, libraries are no longer totally tied to publishing in its traditional form, which may no longer be the most efficient, economical or effective way of storing and disseminating certain types of information. Technology has changed the way that libraries provide information; the end product is made available quickly and comprehensively, and the user does not really care where it is stored or how it is retrieved. This development has enhanced the library's role as an educational institution. Remote access to some of the library's collection will mean that some users will no longer need to visit a physical building called the library and librarians will be performing different, more important, consultative roles either in person or online.

This change from warehouse to supermarket, from a passive role of preserver to an active one of purveyor, has brought greater emphasis on service, identifying needs and communicating solutions, rather than on just the process of lending books.

THE LIBRARY'S MISSION

The term "library" today is a complex one requiring modifiers: *academic,* with the primary educational/research role of scholarly communication in line with the goals and objectives of the larger institution of which it is a part, and with a clientele composed primarily of faculty/researchers and students; *public,* with a seemingly impossible mission of being "all things to all people," yet primarily a "free" informational and recreational institution; *school,* with an integrated educational role within the total curriculum; and *special*, as the key point in the management of information relevant to an organization's growth and development, whether the organization is an insurance company, a medical facility, a law firm, a museum or other institution.

One goal of public and academic libraries has been that of preserving cultural heritage and intellectual resources. Although this traditional role is not likely to change, public libraries must guard against alienation of potential users by becoming simply knowledge storehouses available only to certain segments of society. Libraries have sometimes been typecast as elitist institutions, almost arrogant in their services, offering limited access to resources only to those who can read. The prepackaged print-on-paper form limits library users to this group, while those who cannot read seek information, education and entertainment from other mass media sources such as television. Those who can read have always had the incentive and the advantage in using libraries. Now it must be added that those who can afford to buy information have an even greater advantage, as more and more libraries feel the need to charge fees for special services.

In the current debate over "free vs. fee" based library resources, fundamentals of good library service are being threatened. The rapid advance of technology, while expanding the library's horizons, is at the same time presenting the potential for limiting access, particularly for smaller libraries facing economic hardships. Technology provides broader access to information, but it is not a panacea since it can never substitute for the knowledge process which constitutes the basis of good library and information service. It will never be a substitute for knowledge, but rather an enhancement of the learning process.

Libraries must be prepared to provide a variety of knowledge modes and to recognize the importance of each. Although it is true that print-on-paper is becoming less popular as an information storage and retrieval medium in libraries, and its use as humanity's dominant vehicle of learning has declined as the impact of technology has been felt, its usefulness will not be superseded by another medium. Rather, the variety of media will complement one another to provide an integrated information environment in libraries and will enable libraries to serve a growing proportion of the population.

Identifying User Needs

Traditionally libraries have played a rather passive role in relation to user needs. Users have not expected more, because they have not seen themselves in the kind of "client" relationship that has developed with most other professionals— lawyers, doctors, teachers, social workers. In a study of citizen information-seeking patterns, libraries were listed ninth in the hierarchy of sources consulted.[4] Perhaps this is an indication that few actually cast the library in the role of indispensible information provider and the librarian in the role of diagnostician of information needs. In a more leisurely past, although some libraries were challenged to perform this information role, they were not confronted with the almost chaotic situation that exists today.

Studies show that libraries actually still know relatively little about how and why they are used for informational purposes. All that is known, intuitively, is that needs are growing at a faster pace than the ability to meet them. It appears that those who do use libraries have recognized the limitations of physical access, cost, and sophistication or understandability of information available, and have adapted their use patterns to the library's environment.

Public Libraries

Those seeking information to cope with daily life or to solve work-related problems have not traditionally thought of public libraries as being a primary source for information. This is particularly true for large segments of the population

4. Ching-chih Chen, "Citizen Information Needs—A Regional Investigation," in *Options for the Eighties,* ed. Robert D. Stueart (Greenwich, CT: JAI Press, 1982).

who have limited intellectual skills. To reach these people, libraries must be prepared to offer custom-tailored products, to develop a new educational role as an essential lifelong service and a vital public utility. The call is to serve the illiterate as well as the visually and technologically literate. All kinds of information needed to solve citizen problems must be provided by libraries. Some of it is not found in books.

Libraries are thus offering more and more services to appeal to non-readers as well as the traditional, reading library patron. Movies, musical programs, classes on quilting or karate, career counseling are among many such services. Literacy programs, cosponsored by libraries and other social agencies, are important in the library's efforts to reach a larger constituency.

Increasing numbers of libraries are providing patrons access to the information services offered by microcomputer networks such as The Source and Micronet. These services include news and financial reports, educational programming, household hints and electronic mail.

By bringing more patrons to the library, such services can increase the use of books. This has been shown in the case of film and television programs. For example, television airings of *Brideshead Revisited* and the young adult story *The Summer of My German Soldier* saw libraries inundated with requests for copies of those books. Popular movies have produced similar demands. "Have You Watched A Book Today," mounted by a public television station in Bloomington, IN, brought people to the library in droves. The increased use of video technology through closed circuit television programs produced by public and academic libraries is likely to increase the trend, particularly as people have more leisure time and as pressing educational issues are identified.

Public libraries will continue to provide traditional services—general reference, recreational reading, local history, archival records, basic educational materials. But if they wish to avoid being superseded by other information sources, they can no longer take a passive role in the information/education process. To compete with the for-profit information industry, and to provide services to all those who cannot afford to pay for information, they must become part of the technological revolution. This means that more and more public libraries will offer electronic data base searching, videotext services, and materials available in computer-generated formats such as encyclopedias, indexes and programmmed texts.

School, Academic and Special Libraries

Both the school library/media center and the library/learning resource center in universities and colleges are charged with providing primary and secondary source materials and services to support the curriculum. Certain kinds of heavily used sources in those types of libraries—abstracts and indexes, reference works such as dictionaries, encyclopedias and handbooks which are easily updated—are prime candidates for presentation in electronic form. As such, they have been the first innovations used in libraries as substitutes for the book. These innovations, along with access to online catalogs, have meant that bibliographic retrieval is faster, more efficient and has a greater possibility of being comprehensive. Increased user awareness of such resources will probably generate greater demands for delivery of the print materials themselves.

Another important factor in both academic/research libraries and special libraries is the need for ready access to research materials. Libraries are viewed not only as repositories of such information, but also as facilitators of research, particularly through selective dissemination of information (SDI) services. These services, which alert researchers to new material relevant to their special interests, are particularly effective when offered via online information retrieval systems. A user profile of interests can be stored indefinitely, and data base updates can be searched automatically by computer. The citations are automatically retrieved and mailed periodically to the user. The emergence of electronic mail and other telecommunications technologies is making SDI even more efficient.

Although certain researchers may have access to online search services provided directly by vendors, it is doubtful that they will have either the intuition or the overall searching capabilities necessary to retrieve all materials pertinent to their interests. That is why the role of mediator (i.e., librarian) has become more crucial as information has become inter-disciplinary and diffuse, and access to it has become more difficult. Further, it is unlikely that researchers or other users will be able to subscribe to the wide range of electronically published journals or other necessary materials. Even with computer costs decreasing, it is doubtful that information seekers, other than a relatively few researchers, would have the financial resources required.

The library's role will be amplified as users become more dependent on information professionals as negotiators and as scholars perceive the subject-specialist librarian as one who knows better than anyone else what's good for the user. Librarians will become educators of scholars, scientists and other users in accessing machine-readable resources.

SDI or current awareness services are crucial concerns as libraries struggle with budget limitations and are forced to be increasingly selective in their purchases and user services. Careful collection management is necessary to select the right materials, to discard outdated ones and to guard against the acquisition of useless information. Research-oriented librar-ies must anticipate user needs and ensure that the research materials are available when needed so that research can go forth unimpeded.

RESOURCE SHARING AND ACCESS TO INFORMATION

Information self-sufficiency will not mean that an institu-tion will own everything of potential use. Debate will focus increasingly on how much the institution should own as contrasted to how much it should access materials it does not own when they are needed. Interlibrary borrowing will continue for all types of libraries. In fact, many observers believe that interlibrary loans, along with other forms of resource sharing, must and should increase.

Since World War II the increase in specializations and the explosive growth of published information has seen libraries strained to the seams. Many recent calls for collection curtailment have come not only from funding authorities but also from professionals blazing new cooperative ventures in networking and resource sharing in hopes of developing national systems such as those available through the Washington Library Network (WLN), Online Computer Library Center (OCLC) and Research Library Information Network (RLIN), and through such concepts as the ill-fated National Periodicals Center. In the past, large university libraries had sufficient funds to purchase one copy of everything of potential research value or of leisure/educational interest to their users. The past is gone, and expansionism in ownership is dead.

Moreover, recent research has cast doubt on the idea that the larger the collection the better able it is to perform its educational/research/recreational purpose. There is a fallacy in the argument that the larger the library, the more likely it is to provide immediate access to what is needed. Studies have shown a lower success rate than might have been imagined. Libraries have come to realize that a disproportionate percentage of the book collection is never consulted. Some have postulated that there is a core of materials in the library, perhaps 20%, which serves the majority of needs (or at least of recorded requests). Others have speculated that 40% of the collection may account for almost all of the use. Nevertheless, libraries are under constant pressure to build collections to increase the probability that a particular volume will be accessible when it is needed, even if by only one user.

The primary impact of technology on collections in the immediate future is in the enhancement of resource sharing, which allows libraries to eliminate duplication of materials, particularly those likely to receive infrequent use. This realization has caused some concern among publishers who, in the past, have relied on mass library purchasing. Economic constraints, coupled with the capability of libraries to provide speedy access to lesser-used or shared materials, mean that library budgets can no longer be looked to as sole supporters of some commercial publishers. An uneasy truce has been called while those on both sides dance around that important issue.

Resource sharing, to be successful, requires prompt physical access. Traditionally this access, with only partial success, has been accomplished through the postal service, with the physical document or a copy being sent to the user. In the not too distant past photocopying produced a revolution, particularly in interlibrary lending of periodical materials. Development of telefacsimile transmission devices brought the potential for speedier access. Online access to bibliographic data, available through such networks as OCLC, allows member libraries to know the full holdings of a range of institutions. This simplifies interlibrary borrowing, but also raises questions about "free" access to materials, questions that future library legislation is sure to address in greater detail.

In addition, modern library networks have enhanced libraries' internal operations relating to cataloging, serials and circulation control, and acquisitions procedures. Refinements in computer and communications technologies, including breakthroughs in microcomputer hardware and software, have made bibliographic access and interlibrary loan easier for even the smallest of libraries.

Other technological developments that have allowed wider access to library collections include fiber optics, which make it possible to photograph whole books on single plates, and rapid reproduction and transmission through facsimile. Video discs, on which massive amounts of text and graphics can be stored, indexed and easily retrieved, are being used in some libraries. The Kurzweil reading machine has made written words accessible to the blind. Laser printers and communications satellites have made it easier to produce and transmit huge amounts of information very fast. Interactive videotext services, such as Prestel, developed by the British Post Office, are being tested in the United States. If they are successful, libraries may well be involved in providing information through such sources.

One of the most important needs that has not yet been fulfilled is to provide remote and rapid access to the full-text document for those scholars, particularly scientists, who need it. Although some full text services, such as the LEXIS legal data base, are available, they are not yet affordable. There is no doubt that there will eventually be electronic transmission of textual information at a more reasonable cost. The convenience of online full text will be most attractive to libraries and other information centers in businesses or research institutions that can afford it and have need for that immediacy.

Even without full text, online access to bibliographic and numeric data bases has caused a revolution in the way that libraries provide information. It has been said that online search services are not putting libraries out of business; libraries are putting them in business. Even information brokers—many of them educated as librarians and recognized as experts in information management—are often dependent upon libraries for their information. One problem is that though online data bases have facilitated research and scholarly use of the libraries' collections, at the same time, they have thwarted efficient and effective use because of their file structure. Indexes are not integrated according to the way people use information, but rather by series—e.g., ERIC, INFORM, MEDLINE—forcing users to go from one file to another as they would with printed indexes. One must know what is in the data base before accessing it.

UNRESOLVED ISSUES

The continued development of technology for use in accessing library resources is of interest to librarians, publishers, suppliers of library materials and users of all types of libraries. This concern is evidenced in one of the major resolutions which came out of the 1979 White House Conference on Library and Information Services:

> Whereas recent advances in computer technology for the creation and reproduction of documents can provide substantial reduction in cost, and

> Whereas many emerging technologies are now available in the public domain and could be instrumental in supplementing the flow of an access to information, and

> Whereas, development and use of technical and procedural standards can improve effectiveness and reduce cost and extend the use of library and information services, and

> Whereas effective standards facilitate the exchange of information between public and private sections and that this exchange of information is needed to better support organizational, professional and personal activities, and

> Whereas economical media conversion capabilities are very important;

> Therefore be it resolved, that individuals, organizations, and agencies creating documents and books and generating other information be encouraged to create these materials in machine-readable form in order to decrease the load of retrospective conversion, and

> Be it further resolved, that the federal government direct all federally supported libraries and information services and other appropriate federal agencies to support the development, review and adoption of national and international standards for publishing, producing, or-

ganizing, storing and transmitting information, using established and recognized procedures and institutions, and

Be it further resolved that high priority be given to establishing or extending standards which address hardware and software compatibilities, computer and communications network protocol, and machine readable information, and

Be it further resolved that the private sector be encouraged to participate and to support the development of such standards, and

Be it further resolved that research be funded to develop new technologies that permit convenient and economical media conversion from and to appropriate media. [5]

Some of the concerns evidenced in that resolution point to the fact that technology is a double-edged sword for libraries. On the one hand, it relieves the tremendous pressures on physical storage and shrinking budgets; on the other, it calls into question the role of libraries in the information transfer process. Realistically, electronic technologies will enable libraries to take more materials directly to the users, rather than having the users come to the library. Some of the materials, particularly for scientists, would be available online; others would need to be requested either from the host library or by interlibrary loan.

It must be recognized that the traditional methods of purchasing, processing and shelving printed materials are no longer rapid enough, or comprehensive enough, to meet the increasing immediate needs of scientists and other scholars.

---

5. *The White House Conference on Library and Information Services, 1979: Summary* (Washington, DC: National Commission on Library and Information Science, 1980).

The high cost of materials has forced libraries to consider other means of providing ready access to information. Indications are that although libraries may be spending more on acquisitions, they are adding fewer volumes and subscriptions.

This phenomenon led the Enquiry into Scholarly Communications to conclude that the extraordinary growth in information during the last two decades requires important qualitative change in the way certain scholarly materials are published, disseminated, stored and made available. In the past 10 years the number of periodicals increased by almost 20% and subscriptions by libraries increased by almost 40%, bringing the average institution cost up by more than 120%. In excess of 7000 articles and reports are produced each day for a total of more than 2 million scientific writings per year. It is no wonder, then, that electronic, on-demand information retrieval is an attractive innovation for libraries. The introduction of ADONIS, an experimental plan by several periodical publishers to issue 10 to 15 journals in electronic format, is a welcome first step.

For libraries the ownership of journals or other materials is no longer as important as information access and utilization; the documents are simply becoming a by-product of that information access. The problem for scholars and research workers is how to find out quickly what is already known in the area of their immediate research interest; since information may be contained in a variety of sources, one must search several places—and even then crucial information may be missed. Quick bibliographic and physical access to all of those materials will continue to be a goal of libraries.

CONCLUSIONS

One can speculate on what would happen in a future when there are huge data bases containing all kinds of information, in multiple languages with translation capabilities, easily retrieved in a "user friendly" mode with no requirement for additional input, other than sitting at the terminal, and no additional processing required for retrieving by subject, author, title, keyword or any combination thereof. This scenario envisions an annotated, monolithic, ubiquitous store of information totally replacing all libraries and publishers—perhaps even schools and colleges.

Some would maintain that with the possibility of interactive text editing, ours will be an online community, and the traditional, hierarchical communication information system of author, editor, publisher, vendor, librarian, teacher and reader will be abandoned. What would emerge in its place would be a communications scenario excluding all middle-persons, directly from author to reader. By extension, the reader, capable of interacting with the file, would then become author. In such a view, there would arise a real question as to how 5 or 10 billion people could communicate through an online system so enormous and complex as the one required to achieve this interaction. Society must surely go through several stages before reaching that point, if it is ever reached, and there are several issues to be faced before then.

One of the most important in the near future is the question of control of information. Libraries in most democratic countries have always provided free access to materials on all sides of an issue. Electronic publishing offers the potential for greater control of access, by depriving those who cannot afford to buy computers or to pay others to retrieve infor-mation. Moreover, electronic publishing is an undertaking suitable only for large publishers, who might well eliminate "marginal" material that was not economically viable. Such economic censorship might be particularly likely as large conglomerates develop with holdings in publishing, television, radio, computer software and other communications media and products. In such a milieu, the purpose of libraries could be seriously threatened: in the process of accessing online information, libraries could unwittingly become purveyors of biases, built into a system whose bottom line is profit for the data base producer.

There is also the question of the *quality* of materials in massive data bases. In the past most publishers have maintained that if a book or journal is worthwhile it should be published, and libraries have maintained that if it is worth selecting it should be bought. Librarians—and readers—have relied on the "gatekeeper" role of publishers, a controlled editorial policy that screens the information presented. Electronic publishing, particularly of separate, on-demand articles rather than complete journals, affords the potential for anyone and everyone to place materials in the data base. The retention of acceptance criteria and a system of refereeing thus becomes vital to help libraries in the selection process.

Another issue is a concern for the book itself. Norman Cousins once said that "so long as people value thought, there will be a central place for the written word." Something in the nature of a book defies analysis. This intrinsic value cannot be transmitted to another form. It has its own qualities which transmit wonder and delight. The true book has reason beyond that of conveying information; it is an object to be held, to be admired, appreciated and preserved, for its aesthetic and knowledge purveying qualities. Reading and libraries will not become obsolete; the most direct communications channel for many materials is still from author to book to reader, from one mind to another. The library is likely to remain as a focal point for civilization's knowledge, traditions and cultural accumulation.

The library will survive for other important purposes, as well. It will become a more important link between users and their needs, principle access point for knowledge, information and learning. It will provide both bibliographic and intellectual access to those resources. Professionals working in libraries will be negotiators, identifying needs; facilitators, providing effective search strategies; educators, familiar with the literature in all of its formats; and information brokers, providing current awareness services for the populations they serve. The library's role will be one of integrating the information environment.

Although the term "library" has been used throughout this chapter, it should be noted that it is used as a generic term encompassing services to be provided rather than the constraints of a physical building. It is not a question of the conventional library diminishing in favor of an electronic library, but rather of the central information place being able to augment its holdings with access to information available in other places.

The profiles of different types of libraries, and their use of alternative formats as substitutes for the book in the developed nations of the Western world, will continue to vary according to their primary mission and their users' needs. Special libraries, serving industry, scientific institutions and many of the professions which rely heavily upon up-to-date information, much of it found in loose-leaf reference or journal form, will probably maintain the major portion of the library online. Large academic libraries, with huge retrospective collections and with a wide-interest user group from undergraduate students to historians to scientific researchers, will be partly online with total online access to bibliographic information. Smaller college libraries will have less demand for full-text online materials but will have online bibliographic access and portions of retrospective materials in some form other than print-on-paper. Public libraries will also be mixed, with the larger ones maintaining research collections and offering online search services, and both large and small performing community information service functions requiring outreach through communications technology. School libraries will rely heavily on computer-assisted learning as a part of the integrated educational experience for students.

In this electronic setting, one cannot lose sight of a basic purpose of high technology. As Robert A. Plane, president of Clarkson College, put it, "Use of the computer provides

peers and faculty, time to think and contemplate, time to enjoy the physical world about them and yes, time to read books. Even the most enthusiastic computer user doesn't want to read *Moby Dick* or the *Rubaiyat* on a video display terminal." [6]

This is the dilemma libraries find themselves in today. Libraries, created during a more leisurely past, must modify their objectives and operating procedures to meet new and different demands activated by new technologies, or they will find the prospects of long-term survival rather discouraging. The future rests upon being able to balance past functions with new ones and using evolving technologies to meet knowledge and information needs of users and non-users. Libraries must stand firmly with one foot planted in the past as believers in the future of the book—whether novel, poetry, drama, history, biography, essay or short story—and one firmly in the future as believers in the need to provide mass, rapid, comprehensive and economical access to information for an electronically literate population which depends on their expertise as links between human and machine and ultimately with the knowledge they need to function in and contribute to society.

---

6. Robert A. Plane, letter to the editor, "Books Remain Number One at Clarkson College," *The New York Times*, November 5, 1980.

6

Video Disc Technology and the Book

by Lewis M. Branscomb

The laser video disc is tangible evidence of the ability of electronic media to influence the arrangement, distribution and even the creation of human knowledge in novel ways.

Buckminster Fuller has predicted that the video disc "will be the most important lifesaver of humanity." It has been advertised as "gourmet television," but MIT professor Nicholas Negroponte insists it "has nothing to do with movies. It is a book—a surrogate book," he says. *The Financial Times* of London has called it a "gamble past the point of no return." And yet a trade magazine devoted to the subject has dubbed it "one of the best kept secrets of the twentieth century."

The laser video disc has been under development for nearly two decades but was introduced commercially only in 1978. In size and shape it is identical to the long-playing record. But instead of just music, the video disc contains up to 108,000 full-color images, plus two channels of very high quality (stereo) sound, plus computer programming encoded in the disc. All this information is encoded in the form of pits, or indentations, less than a millionth of a meter long, and laid down in tracks so closely spaced that there are 75 times more of them per inch than on a long-playing phonograph record.

To give you an idea of the precision involved, if each microscopic pit were increased to an inch in diameter, the video disc would measure two miles across. The laser that "plays" the record would fly across the surface at a height of five feet, at a speed of 600,000 miles per hour, and would be able to sense indentations as thin as a dime.

Moreover, the optical video disc has unusual durability. A protective coating prevents damage from handling, scratches, dust and impact. And since the information is read by a light beam, there is no wear when the record is played.

Among the capabilities of the laser video disc that have aroused so much interest are its storage capacity; its durability; its ability to give random access to a specific fact or picture; its ready interweaving of different formats (still pictures, motion, text and sound); its ability to go forward or back, display slow motion or freeze a single frame; and its interactive features, i.e., putting the order in which a program is viewed under the control of the viewer. The random access and interactive features become especially valuable when, as in the industrial/educational version of the laser disc player, a microprocessor is used to control the machine.

It should be noted that competing disc systems, notably the capacitive disc which uses a physical stylus to pick up signals encoded on the disc, lack many of these features. What they have in common with the laser disc is great compactness and portability, as well as the potential for rapid, low-cost replication of finished programs.

Before discussing in detail how these features of the laser video disc can influence the transmission of information, it is important to make explicit the relationship between an information medium and the content that it carries.

THE MESSAGE MATTERS

There is no doubt that the video disc is a technological marvel. But those who claim that it will replace the printed book might pause to consider the role that books have played in shaping and illuminating human experience over the past 500 years. The influence of the book far outweighs its economic impact, given that total sales of the U.S. publishing industry, about $7 billion, work out to only $35 per American per year. Nor can the disc match the book's versatility: the disc and player won't fit in the hip pocket of your jeans; can't be read aloud beside a fresh mountain stream; can't be dog-eared, bookmarked or used to press wild flowers. It may be exciting, but it's not lovable, like a book.

The physical attractiveness and portability of books are a further reason why video discs will not replace conventional bookstores. Even if the day comes when a patron could walk into the store and come out with a disc containing the contents of thousands of books, such discs will coexist with, rather than do away with, printed volumes.

In the same way, video discs will not replace libraries. Anyone worried about the future of these institutions can take heart in the sense of possessiveness patrons feel toward them. Such is their loyalty that even New York City, after more than five years of crisis budgets and cutbacks in service and staff, has been restrained from closing a single one of its 197 public library branches—although it has had to curtail hours at many of them. Queens, in fact, has opened several new ones. Libraries remain, in the words of a *New York Times* article, "a warm, free place to go."

Physically speaking, the book is a means for storing, replicating and transporting text and images assembled by the mind of an author. Since the time of Gutenberg, it has been uniquely useful for this purpose, and has brought into being a wide variety of literary forms and a rich literary tradition. The book is the standard by which all other information media must be judged.

Of all the artifacts of industry, books most effectively sustain our intellectual life. And somehow, despite the temptations of commerce and the limited literary taste of the general public, book publishers have managed to maintain a degree of social responsibility thus far unmatched by any of the new electronic media.

Ultimately, these new media will stand or fall, not so much on electronics and hardware, fascinating as these may be, but on the information that goes into them. More than ever, the quality and value of that information will be the determining factor in the success of cable, direct broadcast satellite, optical fibre, video tape, video disc and computer information services.

An explanation is in order on my use of the word "information." As we all know, information encompasses both wisdom and knowledge, truth and deception, beauty and depravity. Both the electronic media and books span the full range, although many critics have been harsh in their judgment of video electronics. Douglass Cater says, "Karl Marx was wrong. Religion is not the opiate of the masses. It's television."

One advantage in using the computer expression, "software," is that it has the virtue of carrying no implications of value or quality. The nature of the "software" that evolves with the new technologies will determine, for good or evil, their ultimate effect on our lives. McLuhan was only half right. The medium is not the message, but can create new dimensions to the message. It's the message that matters.

As one surveys the extraordinary possibilities of these technologies, the real question is the one uttered by Henry David Thoreau. He was told that a telegraph wire was to be laid between Maine and Texas, and was asked his reaction. What, he is said to have replied, has Maine to say to Texas?

From a technical perspective, the new electronic media provide capabilities going far beyond both books and motion pictures. Clearly the potential is there for genuinely new and unique media. But will the video disc, for example, live up to that potential? Or is it merely a new way for a movie producer to distribute his film—a new way to shuttle about old information?

The answer lies in how creative people use it.

But who will "write" the new video books? Who will construct the electronic encyclopedias? Who will find out what is real and what is gimmick?

THE MEDIUM CAN CHANGE THE MESSAGE

One of the fascinating questions to consider in examining the future of the video disc, or of any new information medium, is whether it can stimulate the development of profoundly new kinds of authorship. Sometimes a new medium does bring forth new creative talent and new forms of art. We think of D.W. Griffith with motion pictures. But we also know from the hard lesson of commercial television that software may not live up to the promise of new technologies for distributing it.

What explains the artistic diversity of film and the moronic dullness of television? Perhaps the answer lies in the few channels traditionally available for broadcasting, a scarcity that has forced an emphasis on programs appealing to the largest possible audience. Since over-the-air television has had no possible economic support except advertising (until the very recent advent of subscription television), programs that might appeal to smaller audiences never have a chance to be aired. Thus, whereas film has given us new cognitive dimensions for viewing the world (compared to the earlier media of print and pictures), TV has primarily added convenience of access—and at the price of poorer visual and auditory quality. As a medium for creators and artists, it is fair to say that television's potential remains to be developed.

The Impact of Gutenberg

The relationship between a medium and creators can be well illustrated by examining a media innovation far earlier than motion pictures: Gutenberg's invention of the platen

press and movable type. It was an invention whose unexpec-
ted results changed the concept of authorship.

For centuries, before the invention of printing, the monastic
institutions engaged in manuscript copying were largely
concerned with a race against time—to replicate copies of
ancient texts before the ravages of time wore out existing
versions. Printing itself was at first a backward-looking
activity. As a 16th century writer put it, "The invention has
greatly aided the advancement of all disciplines. For it seems
miraculously to have been discovered, in order to bring back
to life more easily literature which seemed dead."

The modern-day TV commercial showing Brother Sebas-
tian using his Xerox copier for manuscript replication helps us
understand the irony of Gutenberg's invention: in fact what
Gutenberg was seeking was a mechanical copying machine,
not a printing press. Thus, the impetus for printing was the
more rapid reproduction of pre-existing knowledge. But the
technology also made possible a new set of functions. It
shifted control of the text away from the archivist to the
author.

Within a short time, knowledge came to be perceived as
being subject to a permanent process of augmentation, rather
than merely recovery. Printing, which had been invented to
reduce the labor of copying text, had altered the perception,
and even the nature, of the text itself and its role in society.
Five hundred years later, the traditional medium of our time
—the printed page—has helped to stimulate a far wider range
of information needs and desires than print alone can gratify.

Individualized Information

What can a medium that is selectively accessible under
computer control do for us that books and film cannot?

Like the book, the new electronic media—videotext, satellites, cable and video discs—all have the capability to
individualize information—to make the acquisition of knowl-

edge a matter of private choice. But they do so in a far more dramatic manner.

In a sense, this notion of user-controlled selectivity is not new. There has always existed an audience for information of a specific nature to be delivered according to individual choice from a large aggregation of knowledge. The system that has provided that service for 3000 years is called a library.

Electronics has shrunk that library's archives dramatically, and has extended its reading room to all the people within the reach of antennas, cables or fibres. It has so reduced the cost of storage that in the future, large parts of the library can be replicated economically at the user's location. But the most revolutionary change is the reduction in time from book stacks to retrieval. The electronic book stacks can be searched with the speed at which light travels. You can have a conversation with your electronic library.

The video disc offers an exciting glimpse into this technological phenomenon whereby information acquisition functions that once required the physical surroundings of the library can now be carried out using an electronic surrogate.

WHAT THE DISC CAN DO

We have already listed some of the significant features of the laser video disc, ranging from its storage capacity and durability to its interactive capability. Now let's look at these capabilities in more detail.

Storage Capacity

The video disc and other forms of electronic storage can help us cope with the "information explosion" that seems to be overtaking modern society.

This problem, like so many others which we are facing today, has been neatly anticipated in science fiction. One story, related by Christopher Evans in *The Micro Millennium,* tells how, despite the use of microfilm and other information-compression devices, 90% of the world's surface has had to be given over to data storage, the inhabitants squeezing into a tiny area of living space.

> ...Huge artificial satellites are then employed and in due course, the moon, too, becomes a filing cabinet.
> Hundreds of years pass; information increases remorselessly and so does the storage problem, until all the other planets in the solar system have their surfaces (and interiors) crammed with "libraries" and file warehouses. The story concludes with an expedition across interstellar space in a search, not for adventure or the glory of colonization, but for fresh worlds on which to dump Earth's files and records. On the outbound voyage, however, [the spaceship encounters] an alien spacefleet coming from the opposite direction, so to speak, and on an identical mission.[1]

The laser video disc could postpone that expedition considerably. As mentioned earlier, its two sides can hold 108,000 separate images. In its television version, each image would have to conform to the analog display of a regular TV set, which means a practical limit of 150 words of text; thus such a disc could hold about 36,000 book pages, or 120 books at 300 pages per book. However, there is another possibility. Instead of formatting the disc for playback through a normal TV set, information could be encoded digitally on the disc for display on a computer terminal. In this case, 10 billion bits of digital information per side, used to code the characters in printed text the way a computer does it, would permit storage of 1600 books per side, or 3200 books per disc, each of 300 pages. A 300-page book could occupy the equivalent of a thumbnail-sized area on the disc.

---

1. Christopher Evans, *The Micro Millennium* (New York: Viking Press, 1980).

(It should be pointed out, of course, that a disc encoded in this way could not be played back through the same disc players now on the market to show entertainment and training programs. The players would have to have some additional electronic circuits to handle the digital information.)

Durability and Archival Quality

Equally attractive to libraries, whose contents are not only bulging at the seams but slowly crumbling on the shelves, is the disc's durability. At present, lifetime appears for all practical purposes to be unlimited.

Selective, Random Access

The third power of the electronic, computer-controlled media is selectivity. Given an economical technology for archiving a vast and growing store of information, highly selective access is required.

On the disc one may store images of 108,000 of the world's art treasures, or 108,000 pictures of Jupiter and Saturn taken by the Voyager spacecraft. Each frame on the disc—each picture—has its unique electronic address. You can browse, use an index or go directly to the specific picture you want. The access time to reach any single frame is comparable to that of computer mass storage systems —a few seconds.

Combination of Formats

Other functions of the video disc begin to emerge when we consider that a program author can combine the best qualities of film, full-motion video, animation, slides and print in a single format for convenient presentation. The orchestration and interweaving of those media elements will create a new art form — a new dimension in audiovisual communications that I believe will be greater than the sum of its parts.

For example, encyclopedias in disc format could provide visual, aural and print treatment of a host of subjects, e.g., animals, musical instruments, machines or games. An encyclopedia in the future might consist of fewer volumes and a supplementary series of video discs. The publishers of the Academic American Encyclopedia have already produced a demonstration disc as a prototype. And on a smaller scale Houghton Mifflin is preparing a video disc showing birds in their natural habitat, singing their songs in high-fidelity stereo, to accompany "The Field Guide to the Birds" by Roger Tory Peterson. (Because of the much greater number of video cassette players in consumers' hands, this program will probably be released first on video cassette, even though cassette players do not offer stereo sound.)

The two audio tracks offer additional possibilities beyond hi-fi stereo sound. Dual languages are one obvious use of this capability. Another is presenting two levels of information —tailored to different audiences (such as a surgeon and a surgical nurse)—using the same visual material. One consumer disc, already released, on "How to Watch Pro Football," uses the two-channel stereo to permit simultaneous comments from the offensive and defensive coaches. A quiz on play formations used in the game has the questions on one sound track, the answers on the other.

Variable Speed: Single Frame, Slow Motion, Etc.

Being able to freeze and observe a single frame, and select slow- and fast-motion, forward and reverse, offers still more options. Users of a program being developed by a manufacturer of musical instruments, for example, will be able to stop-frame and slow-motion back and forth to observe the instructor's fingering on a guitar.

Interactive Capability

The use of variable speeds, and the interweaving of formats, are key aspects of what is really the exciting feature of the laser disc: its ability to facilitate user interaction. Interactivity sets the video disc apart from other media. This is what provides opportunity for the hitherto passive viewer to become an active participant—reacting to what he or she sees, directing visual content at a personalized pace. Interactivity opens a vista of application possibilities—and challenges for program authors—limited only by our imaginations.

Previous audiovisual media were, like most books, meant to be "paged" in one direction, one page at a time. For hundreds of years, our printed art forms, music, films and novels have been in linear, time-sequenced formats. Most books have been printed with the expectation that they will be read that way, although "who-dunnit" authors have long known that some readers cheat by reading the last chapter first, and jaded readers have learned from experience that the editors often insert some raunchy stuff around page 85 in otherwise serious first novels. Actually, the newspaper is the most interactive print format, allowing the reader to scan the news vertically or horizontally at his pleasure.

The optical video disc gives the viewer the same degree of control, sequence, pace and starting point that a book provides, including indexing and reference capability. With a hand-held keypad and the player's microprocessor, the viewer has the option to select any chapter, any page, from an index on the screen. And as soon as that segment completes, the program can take you right back to the index, if that's what's wanted.

But this is a one-dimensional form of interactivity, relating to the disc's ability to provide random access. The disc is not like a broadcast TV program or a documentary film that must be viewed from beginning to end in order to have meaning. With the computer logic on the disc, you must think of it as a kind of 3-D newspaper. Behind each headline and story is another whole newspaper, with an electronic editor at your disposal to lead you into the background sections and stories.

Interactivity has obvious entertainment possibilities. The public's initial exposure to interactivity—via their television sets—came with the introduction of TV games. It was their first appreciation of the impact of blending audiovisual techniques with the power of the computer.

Yet another application of the interactive disc is as an electronic salesman or catalog, able to respond to each customer's particular interests. The chances are that most people will first come in contact with an interactive video disc in a General Motors showroom, a department store or a museum or travel agent's office.

For example, the Metropolitan Museum of Art is considering the disc as a supplement to standing exhibits and may even sell exhibit discs through its book shop. Travel organizations are especially interested in a concept called "vicarious travel," originated by Professor Nicholas Negroponte of MIT. Using a "joystick" control to advance the video sequences in either one of two discs on separate players, a viewer can create the sensation of a tour of Aspen, CO, in which he "decides" whether to turn left or right, go forward or backward. The same technique could be applied to visiting the Louvre or hiking the Wilderness Trail. (Needless to say, production of such programs will be extremely expensive. But if they appeal to a wide enough audience they could be sold at a reasonable price. Pretty soon that may be the only kind of travel many of us can afford, anyway.)

Besides its obvious uses in entertainment or shopping, the disc's interactive quality is particularly important in educational applications. Here, the laser disc equipped with a microprocessor can combine the best of computer-assisted instruction and audiovisual techniques. The visual information is presented, and the student may respond to questions and options as he goes along. His scores and response times can be recorded, and a learning profile can be created.

An incorrect answer triggers a branching back to review and remedial sequences that will guide the student. Right answers provide positive feedback. The student is involved in a learning process that uses all of his senses, and he moves at his own pace.

Students at all levels, from elementary school on, could receive instruction via the disc. For example, WICAT Systems has developed a disc on diagnosis and treatment of gastrointestinal disease, for Smith, Kline and French. With an actor playing patient, the viewer—a doctor or medical student—is given his choice of patient history questions, and of laboratory tests and treatments. If the student misses an important point, he is led back for another look. If he orders too many tests, he is chided for wasting time and the patient's money. This disc is a harbinger of a new approach to the author-viewer relationship.

THE CREATIVE PROCESS: READER/VIEWER AS AUTHOR

The capabilities of the video disc portend an exciting future. But I hasten to remind you that in the words of that great philosopher, Pogo: "There is no heavier burden than a great potential." And I am equally convinced that the imagination and justification for the video disc's application must come from forces outside the technology.

Part of the challenge is to create, design and write the new programs that take full advantage of the medium's capabilities. In short, the creative process must catch up with the technology.

Early video disc materials designers have found that they require new ways of approaching the creative task, with access and interaction always in mind. They must work against what seems to be the grain of straight linear process, and think in terms of choices, instead. One wouldn't expect the transition to be easy; after all, we come from thousands of years of linear thinking in the writing of books, plays, movies and television.

Not that books, for example, *need* to be linear. Here is a nonlinear, interactive book—a story called "Your Code Name is Jonah." Actually, it's many stories with 41 different endings. The reader is the detective in a spy story. Throughout the book, the reader is asked to decide which of two or three things he would do next. Each decision directs him to a different page, depending on the answer. Some readers don't find this book very satisfying—especially when they keep ending up in the hospital or dead, which is the outcome about half the time.

Such a book could be coded in digital form on an optical video disc, allowing the reader to explore an extraordinary wealth of alternative outcomes—provided, of course, the author has the persistence to write such a prodigious multi-book. But how will authors feel about crafting their work to put the reader in control? Is that really in the reader's interest —in the interest of good literature?

Once a book is in the hands of a reader, the author is only accessible through his printed words. But assuming the author's time were not at issue, would an author really welcome a conversation with his reader? That is at least debatable.

This vision of the interactive video disc is suggested by the title of an excellent piece by Robert Dahlin in the March 27, 1981, *Publishers Weekly*. He called it, "Consumer as Creator." Dahlin quotes George Rosato of Random House: "The new technologies allow the user to become the publisher. He calls up on his computer screen just what he wants. By tradition, we (publishers) represent the information source, predetermining what it was that the reader would use. Technology now permits the user to have what he wants when he wants it. That is a staggering difference."

Some authors may have some doubts about sharing the creative stage with their readers. An author's talent, invested over a lifetime of observing and writing about the human condition, is not matched by most readers. Indeed, I suspect some of our greatest authors write primarily for themselves.

Flannery O'Connor might have shared that view. She wrote in 1957:

> Ours is the first age in history which has asked the child what he would tolerate learning (in the field of liter-ature)....The English... teacher will be fulfilling his respon-sibility if he furnishes the student a guided opportunity, through the best writing of the past, to come, in time, to an understanding of the best writing of the present....And if the student finds that this is not to his taste? Well, that is regrettable. Most regrettable. His taste should not be consulted; it is being formed.

Using a new technology to communicate efficiently and give the reader/viewer a broad range of choices is one thing. Making an artistic success of it, and using it for the betterment of mankind, are something else altogether.

I worry that the reader of the "electronic books" of the future will choose to sample only the information that he knows he *wants* to know. In many cases, that's probably *not* the information he most *needs* to know.

The problem of excessive information selectivity is already with us; we don't have to wait for the interactive video disc, videotext or several hundred channels on cable and rooftop satellite antennas. It exists in the form of "narrowcasting." Robert Dahlin again (March 20, 1981, *Publishers Weekly*): "Segmenting a market...into smaller specialized groups is called narrowcasting, and narrowcasting is where it will be at, say neophyte electronic publishers, when there is sufficient computer hardware around to insure an audience."

Elie Abel, broadcaster and dean of the Columbia Journalism School, worries about the roots of consensus in a democratic society when everyone listens only to his personalized view of the world. However fragmented our information media become, some voices—publishers, writers, artists—must con-tinue to speak to us in the broadest, most catholic sense.

The outcome lies not in the control of the developers and

suppliers of the technology. After all, we don't blame librarians or press operators for failure to encourage new, experimental writers. The problem goes back to the encouragement society gives—or doesn't give—to the scholar, the author and the artist—as well as to those gatekeepers (publishers, project grant officers, critics and reviewers) who provide the funds and control access to the means of distribution.

WILL CREATIVE PEOPLE SHAPE THE
NEW TECHNOLOGY?

One hears a lot of talk these days about the impact of technology on people. Hardly anyone writes an article or makes a speech about the impact of people on technology.

But in the spring of 1981 actress Kathleen Nolan, past president of the Screen Actors Guild, did just that at the Philip Morris Conference on Communications in the 21st Century. She made some provocative points that are well worth repeating.

Ms. Nolan noted a survey a few years ago that asked children if they had to choose between their father and television, which would they give up? They chose to give up their fathers. That *is* something to worry about.

If our technologies are to be used constructively, in support of our highest ideals, Ms. Nolan suggests that we need to cultivate some new habits: the habit of creative consciousness, the habit of freedom. Just as sheep are in the habit of being sheep, so can humans—the most adaptable of all species —learn to get in the habit of being creative.

Fortunately, Ms. Nolan has identified among us a peculiar subspecies of human that has been around for a long time and can help. Some people would even call this subspecies aliens —perhaps subversives.

This subspecies includes the creative artist, musician, painter, sculptor, scientist, architect and author. And if we don't want to become more and more homogeneous, if we don't want our lives to have less and less content, if we don't want to be a people devoid of emotion—then, Ms. Nolan says, we must allow this creative subspecies to teach us.

Technologists need to be concerned not only with money, but with content and human ideals. And the users of technology need a creative consciousness with which to tell the difference. Only then will we have a choice about what life in the 21st century will be like.

BIBLIOGRAPHY

"Advertising: 1776-1976," *Advertising Age,* April 19, 1976.

Boaz, Martha, ed. *Strategies for Meeting the Information Needs of Society in the Year 2000.* Littleton, CO: Libraries Unlimited, Inc., 1981.

The Business Information Markets, 1980-1987. White Plains, NY: Knowledge Industry Publications, Inc., 1982.

Chen, Ching-chih. "Citizens Information Needs—A Regional Investigation." In *Options for the Eighties*, edited by Robert D. Stueart. Greenwich, CT: JAI Press, 1982.

Compaine, Benjamin M. *The Newspaper Industry in the 1980s: An Assessment of Economics and Technology.* White Plains, NY: Knowledge Industry Publications, Inc., 1980.

——————— *The Business of Consumer Magazines.* White Plains, NY: Knowledge Industry Publications, Inc., 1982.

Evans, Christopher. *The Micro Millennium.* New York: Viking Press, 1980.

Fry, Bernard M., and White, Herbert S. *Publishers and Libraries: The Study of Scholarly and Research Journals.* Lexington, MA: Lexington Books, 1976.

Hill, Philip, ed. *The Future of the Printed Word.* Westport, CT: Greenwood Press, 1980.

King, Donald W.; Lancaster, F.W.; Kenney, Brigitte; et al. *Telecommunications and Libraries: A Primer for Librarians and Information Mangers.* White Plains, NY: Knowledge Industry Publications, Inc., 1981.

Lancaster, F. Winfred. *Toward Paperless Information Systems.* New York: Academic Press, 1978.

O'Neill, Gerard K. *2081: A Hopeful View of the Human Future.* New York: Simon and Schuster, 1981.

Plane, Robert A. "Books Remain Number One at Clarkson College." *The New York Times,* November 5, 1980.

The Print Publisher in an Electronic World. White Plains, NY: Knowledge Industry Publications, Inc., 1981.

Rochell, Carlton, ed. *An Information Agenda for the 80s.* Chicago, IL: American Library Association, 1981.

Scholarly Communications: The Report of the National Enquiry. Baltimore, MD: Johns Hopkins Press, 1979.

Sigel, Efrem, et al. *The Future of Videotext.* White Plains, NY: Knowledge Industry Publications, Inc., forthcoming.

Sigel, Efrem; Schubin, Mark; Merrill, Paul F.; et al. *Video Discs: The Technology, the Applications and the Future.* White Plains, NY: Knowledge Industry Publications, Inc., 1980.

Spigai, Frances, and Sommer, Peter. *Guide to Electronic Publishing.* White Plains, NY: Knowledge Industry Publications, Inc., 1982.

Toffler, Alvin. *The Third Wave.* New York: William Morrow & Co., 1980.

The White House Conference on Library and Information Services, 1979: Summary. Washington, DC: National Commission on Library and Information Science, 1980.

ABOUT THE AUTHORS

Efrem Sigel is editor in chief of Knowledge Industry Publications, Inc. He is editor and co-author of *Videotext: The Coming Revolution in Home/Office Information Retrieval* and co-author of *Video Discs: The Technology, the Applications and the Future* and *Crisis! The Taxpayer Revolt and Your Kids' Schools*. He is also author of *The Kermanshah Transfer*, a novel. Mr. Sigel is a graduate of Harvard College and the Harvard University Graduate School of Business Administration.

Erik Barnouw is professor emeritus of dramatic arts at Columbia University. From 1978 to 1981 he was chief of the Motion Picture, Broadcasting and Recorded Sound Division of the Library of Congress. He is the author of numerous books on the history of the mass media, including *A History of Broadcasting in the United States* and *Tube of Plenty: the Evolution of American Television*. He has been the recipient of the Bancroft Prize in American history, the Frank Luther Mott Award in journalism history, the George Polk Award, the Grand Prix (Vienna) and the Gavel Award of the American Bar Association.

Anthony Smith is director of the British Film Institute, London. From 1960 to 1971 he was current affairs producer for the British Broadcasting Corp. He has written many books on communications including *Goodbye Gutenberg: The Newspaper Revolution of the 1980s* and *The Geopolitics of Information: How Western Culture Dominates the World*. Mr. Smith was educated at Oxford University, England, and was a Research Fellow, St. Anthony's College, Oxford.

Dan Lacy is senior vice president and executive assistant to the chairman at McGraw-Hill, Inc. He is the author of *Freedom and Communications* and *Books and the Future—A*

Speculation, in addition to a number of other volumes. Mr. Lacy is a trustee of The Copyright Society of the U.S.A. and chairman of the Executive Committee of the National Humanities Center. He was a member of the President's National Advisory Committee on Libraries (1966-1968). He holds an A.B. and an A.M. in U.S. history and an honorary Litt. D. from the University of North Carolina.

Robert D. Stueart is dean and professor at the Graduate School of Library and Information Science, Simmons College. He received the 1980 Melvil Dewey Medal for creative professional achievement and the RTSD/Blackwell-North America Award as co-editor of *Collection Development: A Treatise*. He is the author of *Area Specialist Bibliographer*, co-author of *Library Management* and co-editor of *New Horizons for Academic Libraries*. A graduate of Southern Arkansas University, Dr. Stueart holds an M.L.S. from Louisiana State University and a Ph.D. in library and information science from the University of Pittsburgh.

Lewis M. Branscomb is vice president and chief scientist of International Business Machines Corp. Previously he was director of the National Bureau of Standards. Dr. Branscomb is chairman of the National Productivity Advisory Committee's Subcommittee on Research, Development and Technological Innovation. He is also a director of Mobil Corp. and General Foods Corp., and a trustee of Vanderbilt University. A graduate of Duke University, he holds an M.S. and a Ph.D in physics from Harvard University.

Other Titles from Knowledge Industry Publications

The Print Publisher in an Electronic World
ISBN 0-914236-81-4   softcover   260pp. $95.00

Guide to Electronic Publishing
by Frances Spigai and Peter Sommer
ISBN 0-914236-87-3   softcover   163pp. $95.00

The Future of Videotext
by Efrem Sigel et al.
ISBN 0-86729-25-0   hardcover 190pp. (approx.) $32.95

Video Discs: The Technology, the Applications and the Future
by Efrem Sigel, Mark Schubin, Paul F. Merrill et al.
ISBN 0-914236-56-3   hardcover 183pp. $29.95

The Book Industry in Transition: An Economic Analysis of Book Distribution and Marketing
by Benjamin M. Compaine
ISBN 0-914236-16-4   hardcover 235pp. $24.95

The Business of Consumer Magazines
by Benjamin M. Compaine
ISBN 0-86729-020-X   hardcover 197pp. $32.95

Birth of Electronic Publishing: Legal and Economic Issues in Telephone, Cable and Over-the-Air Teletext and Videotext
by Richard Neustadt
ISBN 0-86720-030-7   hardcover 144pp. (approx.) $29.95

Telecommunications and Libraries: A Primer for Librarians and Information Managers
by Donald W. King, F.W. Lancaster, Brigitte Kenney, et al.
ISBN 0-914236-88-1   hardcover 184pp. $32.50
ISBN 0-914236-51-2   softcover $24.50

The Library and Information Manager's Guide to Online Services
edited by Ryan E. Hoover
ISBN 0-914236-60-1   hardcover 270pp. $29.50
ISBN 0-914236-52-0   softcover $24.50

Available from Knowledge Industry Publications, Inc., 701 Westchester Ave., White Plains, NY 10604.